THREE
MILE
MAN

THREE MILE MAN

a countryman's
view of nature

Text by Alan Thornhill
Photographs by Peter Warnett
Introduction by Malcolm Muggeridge

with drawings by Lawrence Easden

Collins · London

Acknowledgements

Anyone who attempts to write about the history of
Rotherfield must, of necessity, draw freely on the
work of the late Catherine Pullein, archaeologist
and historian, whose work *Rotherfield. The story of
some Wealden Manors* is a treasury of research and
erudition. I have certainly benefited from her book
and am grateful to the publishers, the Courier
Printing and Publishing Co. Ltd. of Tunbridge
Wells, for permission to do so.

Peter Warnett would also like to thank the many
farmers and landowners around Rotherfield who
have given him permission to follow his life's
hobby on their property.

A.T.

First published 1980
Text © 1980 Alan Thornhill
Photographs © 1980 Peter Warnett
Introduction © 1980 Malcolm Muggeridge
Drawings © 1980 Lawrence Easden
ISBN 0 00-219094-x
Designed by Brian Rockett
Typeset in Garamond by Jolly & Barber Ltd, Rugby
Colour separations by Adroit Photo Litho Ltd, Birmingham
Printed in Great Britain by
Wm. Collins Sons & Co Ltd, London and Glasgow

Contents

Introduction

My first acquaintance with Peter Warnett came about through my grandchildren, on whose behalf he organised a visit to some badgers with whom he had established friendly relations in the woods near the East Sussex village of Rotherfield where he lives. The children had never seen a badger before, and were particularly enthralled to find that badgers shared with them a fondness for peanuts and smarties. Refreshments were provided by Alan and Barbara Thornhill – Peter Warnett works half a day a week in their garden – who also arranged for us to see Peter's superb photographs of the mysterious, beautiful life that still goes on in the countryside round Rotherfield, despite the lorries that thunder through the village, the TV aerials bringing the villagers pictures of the world and its woes, and other intimations of technological progress. My seeing those pictures then, and talking of them later with my publisher helped to set the wheels in motion for Peter's pictures to be published and for this book to be created.

Talking about this most pleasurable badger expedition afterwards, Alan made a point which interested me very much. He had grown up in Rotherfield, where his father was rector for a number of years. Yet, he said, Peter's revelation of the flowers and the creatures and the foliage to be seen in its surroundings filled him with wonder and delight. His circumstances, materially considered, were far superior to Peter's from the point of view of finding the time and the means to explore and study the local countryside. Nonetheless, he had remained blind to much of what Peter saw. Peter had the eyes to see and the ears to hear, whereas Alan's were then differently focused and tuned.

Pursuing this idea, I ask myself whether, with the majority of people getting their impressions of nature from a television screen rather than from life – just by pressing a button or fiddling with a knob – there

would in the future be Peter Warnetts, assiduously, patiently, know-
ledgeably, seeking out, watching and photographing the birds and
insects and animals and flowers and trees which have, through past
centuries, been so important an element in our environment, artisti-
cally and in all sorts of ways. Moreover, as the motorways and the
airways go on expanding and multiplying, and the pesticides go on
being used in ever larger quantities, and the trees go on being cut down,
and commuters turn more and more villages into dormitories, etc. etc.,
will there be any countryside left for a Peter Warnett of the future to
cherish and survey from season to season and from year to year?

Well, if unhappily it should be so – and I think it well may – all the
more reason for being thankful that Peter's pictures have been so
carefully selected and reproduced in THREE MILE MAN, and that in
Alan Thornhill's text his character and outlook and style have been so
skilfully and sympathetically portrayed. He emerges altogether as a
very interesting and attractive person – laconic, shrewd, patient and
perceptive; more in the vein, I should have said, of William Cobbett
than of our twentieth century. I like very much his refusal to com-
promise his standards, though sticking of necessity to his own largely
home-made apparatus, which yet has produced such truly remarkable
results. He refuses to emulate the patter of a media countryman – I am
thinking of one or two regulars in the old days on *Any Questions* – or
otherwise lend himself to dishing up Rotherfield and its environs as
tourist fodder.

The truth is, of course, that in the truest and best sense of the word,
Peter is an artist, with a dogged love for a way of life and its natural
surroundings that our technology and the values it inculcates, are
rapidly destroying. As a naturalist, he is more Wordsworthian than
Darwinian. The contemporary mind seeks to master and dominate
nature, to bulldoze it into meeting all our material requirements; to
fertilize it into becoming ever more fruitful; to get more and more
out of it, whether crops or minerals or flesh – growing flesh greedily
without reference to the ways or even physical shape of the animals
concerned. Peter's attitude is different; he wants to get to know nature
rather than to master it, to accept thankfully what it has to offer rather

8

than, as in a factory farm, distorting nature to meet our appetites. The New Testament tells us that there is concern in Heaven even over a sparrow that falls to the ground. What, then, must there be over a factory farm, the prototype of contemporary husbandry?

Peter Warnett tells how, as a serving soldier in Italy, in the Second World War, he developed a great distaste for being shot at. So, when he got home and was demobilised, he put away his gun and acquired a camera, assuming that the animals he would have hunted might be expected to have the same sort of distaste for being shot at as he had himself. Thereafter, earning a modest but adequate livelihood as a jobbing gardener, he devoted his spare time to studying and photographing his neighbourhood and neighbours other than homo sapiens. I feel sure that future social historians concerned with us and our times – always assuming there are any such – will be interested in a man like Peter as he emerges from the pages of THREE MILE MAN; conveyed therein both by his own pictures, and in his account of how and why he produced them as retailed by Alan Thornhill. Also that there will be many now alive who will get a renewed sense of how precious is our English countryside, from Peter's love and concern for it, and how necessary it is that it should be protected.

Peter does not set out to teach or to instruct, though he is happy to share his knowledge and his secrets with those who know how to treat the countryside and its creatures with due respect. However, from these pages the reader may learn how best to find and study living things. The area around his home on which Peter has concentrated his attentions may differ in terrain and habitat, in flora and in fauna, from the reader's own locality but, in its interest and variety, it is a microcosm of our islands. Peter's greatest accomplishment, perhaps, is that his own patience and skill will inspire others to enrich their lives with a deeper understanding and concern for the wildlife of their own neighbourhoods. I feel sure that this book will open *your* eyes as Alan Thornhill tells us Peter opened his.

Robertsbridge 1980   MALCOLM MUGGERIDGE   9

The Three Mile Man

IT is hard to describe the place where you were brought up as a child, for then you needed no more to describe your surroundings than to describe your mother or father. They were there. You accepted them. You were part of them. Even now, in later life, I feel like saying simply "Rotherfield is a pleasant, mellow Sussex village, horribly overrun by traffic, but otherwise fairly unspoilt by too much urban development." It lies in the north-eastern corner of Sussex, forty-five miles south of London, well outside the stockbroker belt, and a short forty-minute drive to Beachy Head and the sea. Tunbridge Wells and Kent are only seven miles away. To the west, beyond Crowborough, is the great heathland of Ashdown Forest, a forest largely without trees which were stripped to furnish the forges and furnaces of the old iron industry. Cobbett describes Ashdown as "verily the most villianously ugly spot I ever saw in England." Now it seems welcoming and attractive, especially when the sun is out and heather and gorse in full bloom. There is a touch of romance and mystery about it too. It is Winnie the Pooh country, made familiar around the world by Ernest Shepard's drawings.

Rotherfield is a large parish with some 1750 inhabitants. It is part of the Sussex Weald, a varied, hilly, wooded countryside which in ancient times was one vast, almost impenetrable forest, called by the Saxons Andredswald, and which is now a mosaic of villages, small farms, discreet country estates, streams, winding country lanes and the wood and forest land it has always been. Roman roads managed to penetrate the forest but they never cut through Rotherfield. Ours are the narrow twisting country roads of Chesterton's lines:

> Before the Roman came to Rye or out to Severn strode,
> The rolling English drunkard made the rolling English road.

However, it was not drunks, but more likely a respect for property, or the faithful following of streams, that shaped our winding Sussex byways.

The village is mentioned in Domesday Book and its recorded history reaches back even earlier. In an ancient deed dated "In the year of our Lord's Incarnation 792" the local nobleman describes how:

> by the just judgement of God, I, Bertoald, duke, fell into a sickness of which none of the doctors was able to heal me. But I heard that in Gaul, at a monastery of the holy martyrs Dionysius, Rusticus and Eleutherius . . . many miracles had happened through those saints, and getting a safe conduct from the Emperor the Lord Charles I, I came thither. There, after I had prostrated myself to the memory of those saints, I . . . was completely healed. Therefore I vowed an offering to God and those saints . . . and in their names I built a church on my estate in the property called Ridrefeld . . .

So our church today is one of the few in England dedicated to St Denys (or Dionysius), the patron saint of France and one of the martyrs commemorated on Montmartre in Paris, where he was cruelly tortured and beheaded around the year AD 270.

In Bertoald's days Rotherfield must have been an agricultural clearing in the middle of dense forest, the kind of community which King Alfred meant when he wrote that out of a forest "many a fair tun may be built where men may live merrily and softly, summer and winter." The name appears in a dozen spellings: Revedfelle in Domesday Book, Retherfeld, Razelfeld . . . Rotherfield seems to have been settled for only at the beginning of the eighteenth century. It probably means "the open country where the horned cattle feed," for a rother is a horned beast, bull or cow – it crops up elsewhere in the use of rothermarket for cattle market.

I first came to Rotherfield as a child and it was my home during all my school and college days from 1913, when my father became rector of Rotherfield, until his retirement in 1929. Here I grew up with the far from rich, yet privileged and sheltered, life of a parson's son, until my work took me to a busy parish in south London, to a Chaplaincy and Fellowship in an Oxford college, and then far afield in distant lands. At the end of the 1960s I returned to Rotherfield and here, amid the familiar haunts of my boyhood, I have lived ever since.

The village has not changed very much since I was a boy. Worst has been the coming of the juggernaut lorries, which threaten to shake down the old cottages as they make the sharp turn from Station Road, and the increased traffic which would make it dangerous to run a home-made wooden trolley down the gentle slope of South Street as my sister and I often used to do, steering the wheels with reins of string. Our road now boasts a few street lamps, the gravel has given way to tar and the ditch that used to run along it is filled in to make a footpath, but between the houses there are still open meadows where cattle graze. In the spring the road is ablaze with flowering cherry and in early summer with pink and white chestnut and a glorious pink hawthorn.

There have been losses. The blacksmith's forge has gone, the saddler's shop, once an inn called *The Three Guns* because its three ornamental chimneys are shaped like guns, is now a smart greengrocer's – though kept by the family of the original saddler and with the chimneys restored to their former glory as one of the landmarks of the village. One grocer's shop, where there used to be three or four, now supplies most of the villagers' needs and is the centre for all the news and gossip. The old bakery has become a private house (a big inglenook fireplace was discovered behind where the baking ovens used to be).

Although many new houses have been built in Rotherfield few of their inhabitants find employment in the village, which once saw a very varied industry. In the eighteenth century there were notable clocksmiths in Rotherfield: a grandfather clock survives inscribed "Hoadley, Rotherfield" and you can still see the name of "Puttick – watchmaker" written on a wall, but there is no watchmaker today. At the bottom of our garden relics of a clay-pipe factory have been found and brickmaking was also a local industry – remembered in the name of Brickyard Lane. Shingling and tanning were carried out in the village and weaving is remembered in the name of Tenter Meads, where cloth was stretched and dried. An old man who made the wattle sections for penning sheep died only the other day and in my young days I remember charcoal burning.

But the changes in the village are small compared with the difference in the way I now see Rotherfield and the life around it. How blind and self-absorbed I must have been during my boyhood and my youth! I scarcely noticed the gentle Wealden countryside around me and ignored the hazel catkins of the early spring, the cow parsley and buttercups that follow, the scabious and knapweed, the blackberries, the berries of the lords and ladies and the old man's beard. The winding lanes were to me the tracks on which I graduated from a bicycle to my first motorbike, from pony trap to an early family model-T Ford. The only creatures that interested me were the butterflies and moths which I pursued avidly with home-made butterfly-nets. I scrambled over the countryside with a bottle in my pocket, bought from a local chemist for a shilling or two, which probably contained enough cyanide to wipe out half the village. Yet even this interest waned when one day I saw a beautiful creature, pinned out on my setting board, still wriggling a little and I realized that never again could I enjoy killing any living creature.

It was not until I had most of my life behind me and I returned to Rotherfield that I began to understand how my father could say, when we returned from our first Swiss holiday, that, much as he loved the grandeur of the Alps, he loved still more the little hills and valleys of comfortable, comforting Sussex. Now I grudge missing a single month, or even a week, of the changing seasons, of the bare branches picked out with hoar-frost tracery, of crocuses giving way to daffodils, of bluebells to bracken, of the first cuckoo and the last rose!

This change was not brought by maturity. My realization of the wonder of the natural world around me I owe mainly to one man, to Peter Warnett, who, by sharing his knowledge and his enthusiasm has awakened a real interest in nature not only in me but in many other villagers and friends. All his life he has studied the plants and animals of this part of Sussex and has made a hobby of photographing them. He is the true author of this book for it presents his pictures, his knowledge and, mostly, his very words. Getting to know him opened my eyes to an entirely new world.

My sister and I "inherited" Peter, along with the charming house in which she, my wife and I now live. He tended the garden for the maiden aunts who left it to us and he still comes once a week to keep it tidy. For me discovering nature with Peter began at our own front door. When we came here from London we brought two handsome bushes, from our Charles Street roof garden, and planted them in a shady spot close to the house.

"They're nice," said Peter, "but you won't get any berries like that. Those are *Skimmia japonica*, but they are two females. Now I work for a lady who's got two males. We'll do a swop around and get them matched up properly."

Soon arrived a handsome male. It was not long before our remaining female broke out into sprays of glorious berries.

In our village, as in so many others, it takes a while to be accepted as truly belonging. John Brough, our village barber until his death, told me once that after he had been cutting hair in the village for fifteen years one of the real old-timers came in for his regular trim and said: "Well John, how do you like it here?" John replied that he liked it very well. "Are you thinking of staying?" the old timer then asked.

Peter has lived in Rotherfield for forty years but still refers to himself as a "foreigner," although he came from only six miles away. Today, there is no more familiar sight in Rotherfield than Peter Warnett on his bicycle, upright and sturdy, weather-worn and sun-tanned, cap on head, satchel or maybe a camera slung over his shoulder, riding for the so-many-thousandth-time down to the village or out to the woods. There he is on his way to tend a garden, or to repair radios and television sets in a local shop, or out in the long summer evenings to see his family of badgers, or up early to record a bird song, or to photograph a kingfisher flying in to feed its young. He draws his pension now and his time is his own to pursue his life's hobby, rain or shine, summer or winter. He is always on the look-out for that rare flower or unfamiliar bird or butterfly, carefully noting the changes from year to year, from season to season, as old oaks or beeches are cut down, new firs and spruce planted, as the nightingales or the corncrakes disappear, or the tree pipits or the reed buntings come and nest in the thick new foliage.

He has the look of a man who knows just where he is going and yet he seldom seems in a hurry. There is a rhythm of the countryman in the way he manicures a hedge, or coaxes a recalcitrant mower into life. He has time to stop and chat, but his eyes and his ears are ever alert.

Peter is younger than I am and I did not know him as a lad, but I remember his cousin Willie Warnett well. We sang together in the choir long ago. One hot Sunday morning I fainted. "You're just a bit swymey" he said in local Sussex dialect as he laid me out on a nice cool tombstone to recover. Willie also had a sharp pair of eyes. When he was digging in his garden at Longcroft Cottages he found a flint that clearly was artificially formed. It now rests in the Brighton Museum and is described as a "cutter" or "scraper" of the Neolithic age. I suppose it dates from the beginning of Rotherfield's history.

"I don't know much about where we Warnetts come from originally," Peter told me. "My daughter Carol's a librarian and she's got some of it figured out. I believe we were quite well off people in the old days. They say we got on the wrong side in Cromwell's time and the family ran away over to France, where there are 'Warnittes' still. One of 'em must have come back. All I know of my family we've been country folk. The name Warnett may have come from 'warren-netters'. The warren is the place where rabbits were bred, and then netted for food.

"My schooling was in the nearby village of Tidebrook. There weren't many of us young 'uns. The school was kept by a tiny little man and his great big wife. If any of us gave him any trouble, he'd tap on the sliding door, and she'd come in and throw us over a desk and give us six of the best with a copperstick. If you made any fuss, it was a case of 'I'll give you another six.' We've gone too far the other way now. It didn't do me any harm. You had your cane and forgot about it. I left school when I was thirteen. My real schooling has been in the woods. I reckon I've spent half my life among the trees."

Peter was born in a cottage in the woods near Wadhurst called "Fox in the Wood". His father was a woodsman and, as soon as he was old enough, Peter joined him and his two elder brothers working the woods of the Rother valley. The timber company supplied them with a caravan which would be towed to where the felling was to be done and every Monday they would walk or cycle out to it. In summer they would work from four in the morning until nine at night, sleeping in the caravan until Friday.

In winter, working hours would be shorter and the job, paid for by piece-rates, less profitable, so they would stay until Saturday night. It was tough work, swinging a $4\frac{1}{2}$-pound axe all day or keeping up with three full-grown men on one end of a big double saw for an hour or so without stopping. He learned to push hard down on the empty saw as the others drew it back so as to slow them down and make them tired. But there were good times with it all.

At first, Peter was the kettle boy. It was his job to walk to some neighbouring shops for supplies, then to light a fire, cook bacon rashers stuck on hazel twigs, and boil old-fashioned billycans for tea or cocoa. The plants and animals, the sights and sounds of the countryside were the natural background to Peter's life. He was aware of them, as he himself recalls, from his very earliest years.

"One of the first things I can remember is lying on my back under a willow tree, listening to a nightingale singing just above me in the branches. The countryside was full of nightingales then. Then I remember when I was about three, a lady next door pointing out to me the sound of the cock chaffinch. 'Ask it what colour its breast is?' she'd say. And when I did, the male bird would give its usual call '*Pink – Pink*'. And that's what the colour of its breast is, pink.

"You go on learning and listening all the time. I learned a lot from my older brother. Out in the woods with him, he'd point out everything. Among other things, he was a mole-catcher. Women who'd made extra money on munitions in the war liked mole-skin coats in those days. I'd help my brother set his traps and collect the moles. With the money he made he'd save up and buy nature magazines. They came out every week and at the end of the year you could bind them up and make a regular encyclopedia of all sorts of nature.

"We were rabbit catchers too in the old days. Me and my brother would go out with ferrets and nets. The landowners paid us four pence halfpenny a rabbit. On Sundays we would do the same thing for ourselves – poaching. That was more fun than the business side of it – dodging keepers and the like.

"I was only caught the once. It was the first time we went out on a Sunday morning. I was supposed to be in Sunday School and Church. That's where my Mother thought I was. It wasn't for the sake of religion. It was so as the rich people would see you there. If you didn't go to Church, they might take it out on you. It was all part of touching your cap to the gentry when they went by. Anyway, that Sunday morning we weren't touching no caps. We were out with a ferret and half-a-dozen nets. It's a good feeling, more interesting than chasing girls. But we'd only got one rabbit, when the old keeper suddenly showed up. I was only eleven or so, and I was scared. I said something about how we'd only got one rabbit.

"That's where I made a mistake. I shouldn't have let on that we'd got one. So we gave him the rabbit, and then my two brothers gave him sixpence each; that was a week's pocket money. And we hoped he wouldn't let on. But the old keeper went straight to the pub where our Dad was having a lunchtime drink, and told him. I don't know what Dad gave him to keep quiet, but I know what he gave us. 'So you've got caught poaching' he said. Off come his big heavy army belt, and we each got a hiding. 'Remember' he said 'that's not for poaching. That's for getting caught.' And I never got caught again.

"It was a serious matter getting caught. I've never eaten a pheasant in my life. You could get three months in gaol if you touched a pheasant. There were all sorts of summonses. Banging off a gun on a Sunday was an offence of itself. So it was for carrying a ferret. If you hadn't permission for where you'd been, you'd be in Court. 'In search of conies' was the legal term, I believe. I remember going on my bike right past the police at Mark Cross Magistrates Court. I had a ferret in my pocket. Just as I was passing them, I felt something up round my neck, and there was the old ferret sitting right up on my shoulder. They never spotted me.

"An old gentleman I worked for gardening, gave me his gun. That was before the war. But I never used it after. You see I was seven years in the Army during the war. I was in Crete, Greece, Italy, went up the whole length of Italy on foot chasing the Germans. They were running too fast for us to catch them then. By the end of the war I was at an Eighth Army Headquarters, on guard on Christmas Day outside the Schoenberg Schloss in Vienna. It was freezing and snowing six inches already. The General come along with a whole bunch of Officers and said 'Well you can write home and tell your folks that you're having a white Christmas.'

"But, getting back to the gun, you see in the War I got shot at. I durned nearly got my whole shoulder shot right off in Italy. When

I got back home, I thought about that. I didn't like being shot at. Nor do the birds and animals, I reckon. So I gave my gun away.

"After that I'd go out bird and animal watching just for the fun of it. Then, a long time later, I went to some nature talks with colour slides and decided I'd get a camera and have a go. That was about fifteen years ago.

"I got one or two slides and showed them to the local Camera Club. They were good, although I say it myself. Of course the experts just sort of ta-tahed it, called it beginner's luck. When I took another roll, with about fifteen out of twenty good, they had to take notice, didn't they? Later I made a bit of money giving shows and that, and bought a telephoto lens. But most of the stuff I made, such as a remote control gadget so that I could stand away from the camera and operate from there. Later still I made a more elaborate system for taking birds such as kingfishers flying past at high speed.

"I do know a little bit about electronics. In fact that was my hobby long before I took up photography. Of course I've never been able to afford all the elaborate equipment that the professionals use: lenses

costing hundreds of pounds and expensive flash, worked with computers and the like. After all, a gardener's job is about the worst paid going. I've just had a six-pound flash gun, which I dodged up to one eight-thousandth of a second. You know, 'experts' are always telling you that there are certain things you just can't do. This annoys me. 'You can't do this, and you can't do that.' Well, I started out with crystal sets and simple one valve radios. Many a day I've spent fishing listening to a home-made radio with an aerial rigged up in the trees, and a wire down into the water for my earth. Later I built TV sets. So all that has come in handy in building my own gadgets. You do a lot by guess work – and you learn as you go.

"So far as the pictures are concerned, I just aim to take as much as I can of the wildlife, the flowers, the trees, the birds and the animals and all the rest within a three-mile radius of Rotherfield church. Well, I've no transport have I, except my old bike. Besides I got the idea people might be interested to know how much can be seen within three miles of one Sussex village. People who travel all over the place, abroad and such like, often miss what's going on right under their own noses. So, you see, I'm just a three mile man."

Peter's words reminded me of Gilbert White, author of *The Natural History of Selborne.* At the beginning of his famous book are inscribed these words:

> Men that undertake only one district are much more likely to advance natural knowledge than those that grasp at more than they can possibly be acquainted with: every kingdom, every province, should have its own monographer.

I cannot help feeling some affinity with Gilbert White. He too was a parson, brought up in a country rectory and elected a Fellow of his Oxford college. He too returned to his native village to make his home there. But I am an ignoramus. It is Peter Warnett who is our local naturalist and Rotherfield's monographer.

Peter's Patch

THE GLORY of Rotherfield village is St Denys' church. Duke Bertoald's Saxon building was probably made of wood and no trace of it remains, nor of the priory which he founded at the same time. The magnificent church which stands on its site today dates from about 1200, with a massive tower built in the fifteenth century and a shingled spire added later. The inside walls of the entire church were originally a blaze of colour for in 1893, while restoration work was being carried out, a fall of plaster in the nave revealed paintings hidden underneath and frescoes have now been uncovered over the chancel arch and in other parts of the church. A fine Jacobean pulpit and a beautifully carved font are among St Denys' other treasures. A much more ancient font was discovered by a former rector in a farmyard, being used as a trough for pigs. Realising what it was, he made an offer and bought it for five shillings.

Sunday by Sunday, worshippers can see the bellringers at work as the splendid peal of eight bells rings out over the parish, which once included the neighbouring hamlets of Mark Cross and Jarvis Brook and the sprawling and now thriving town of Crowborough. Built on a higher hill than ours, that town was much longer neglected and described as late as the sixteenth century as "the Lord's waste called Crowborough".

As a boy I loved to climb the tower of Rotherfield church. Steep stone steps, corkscrewing up in a sharp, dark spiral, past doors leading off first to the bell-ringers' gallery, then to the chamber containing the big clock, and on beyond the ghostly belfry with its eight bells hanging silent, waiting to be swung into life. Finally, breathless after more than an hundred steps, you can crawl through a low doorway and out into the bright sunlight and stand upon the battlements of our medieval tower, from which you can see all of Peter's three-mile territory and, on a clear day, far beyond towards the long lines of the North Downs on one side and the South Downs on the other.

Stand first on the north side – beware of giddiness, for the lower parts of the battlements are not as high as you might wish! You can look straight down on the old churchyard with a gnarled and splendid yew that may be older than the church itself. Now it seems no more than a mere skin with heart and body eaten away. The tree is propped up with thick wooden supports and yet it still lives on. Somewhere, somehow, it draws life from the rich loamy soil around it and its thick foliage is green and fresh and strong.

Beyond the shops and houses that form the nucleus of the village is the wide expanse of the Recreation Ground. Part of it was once a slaughter house, but now it is as fair a setting as you could wish for village cricket and football. Past farmland that was hop gardens in my young days, are Rotherfield woods, where the oaks and beeches and the coppiced chestnut and hazel mix with the more newly planted firs and pines. In the woods the land falls sharply away, as it does on three of the four sides of the church tower, down through the trees to Redgate Mill, where one of our streams runs down to the Medway.

Move round to the east. Rows of rust-tiled cottage roofs, two old pubs (there are five in the parish altogether – one, the King's Arms, said to be haunted), the manor house and the road down to Rotherfield station carry the eye to a patchwork of meadow and farm. An oasthouse or two stand as a reminder of the hop fields where my mother, my sister and I made some pocket money by joining the London east-enders who came down to work as hop-pickers when the crop was ready. Hops are no longer grown here as a crop but they can still be found straggling over hedgerows here and there. Lush gardens with plenty of trees hide many of the houses. Their flowers attract the butterflies, and their shrubs and undergrowth shelter many a hedgehog, vole and other small animals.

On the lower ground, where the railway used to run, there are small streams, remnants perhaps of the greater rivers that in distant ages helped to carve out our landscape. The farms have somewhat changed their character in this part of the country. Apart from hops, there used to be kale and corn and wheat. You could stir up a pheasant as you walked by. A local farmer once shot a stag on his land, its companions dashing for safety, jumping the hedges like steeplechasers. On a sudden isolated hill, a little to the south, stands a fine windmill which together with another magnificent mill at Mark Cross (destroyed by fire in 1911 and now converted into a private house) and Redgate watermill, shared the grinding of our local corn. But there is little grain harvested around Rotherfield today. The small, divided fields are not suitable for the big machinery used in modern arable farming and local farms are almost all dairy-based. Traffic in our crowded village street must halt from time to time to make way for a flock of sheep or a herd of cattle being slowly driven from one pasture to another. Looking east now, towards the small hamlet of Mark Cross, you can see a healthy pig farm and perhaps some fine Jersey heifers in the fields.

When I looked south, in the old days, the first thing I would have seen from the tower would have been Rotherfield's village green, the Court Meadow, a fine open space where fêtes and fairs were held and villagers came before the lord of the manor to air their grievances or be fined for their misdemeanors. Alas, Court Meadow exists no longer: the pond on which we skated has been drained and the home farm has swallowed it up in sheds, machinery and mud. To the south of the church the land steadily rises – the only side on which it does not fall away. Here too, there are many more private houses than there used to be, but most are hidden away amid thick plantations of wood and variegated hedgerows both of the tamed and untamed variety, many of which must be centuries old. Hedges and roadside banks are rich reserves of nature. Amid the hazel and beech, may and blackthorn, you will find blackberry and wild rose, holly and honeysuckle. Hedges in many parts of the country are being rooted up to make way for modern farming but most of ours remain.

The majority of our meadows are cleared for grazing but I know one farmer in the district who always leaves one of his fields alone until after the cowslips have seeded so that they will continue to be there for anyone to enjoy.

On Cottage Hill, one of the highest points in Sussex, rise many springs, flowing in three different directions: eastward down the Rother to Rye, southward to join the Ouse and north to merge into the Medway. Some of our brooks are a rich rusty colour, the pigmentation caused by the iron carried in the water from the veins of ore it has passed over. The Weald was once the centre of a major iron industry. The round ponds, with traces of forges and furnaces, are still to be found. Not only firebacks and graveslabs were made of Wealden iron but domestic pots and pans and, in Elizabethan times and after, iron cannons for the navy. Ralph Hog of Buxted, a neighbouring village, cast the first-ever iron cannon in the year 1543.

To the west of Rotherfield you look out over the more modern

parish cemetery, set amid meadows, where many a burial has been sweetly disturbed by the lowing of cattle or the bleating of sheep. Beyond this the land slopes steeply down to the more industrialised and suburban valley of Jarvis Brook, and then up again to the ever-spreading town of Crowborough. On this side of the tower there is a platform for a beacon once used for sending urgent news across the county.

The northern part of the Sussex Weald, in which Rotherfield is set, is green and undulating country, offering a variety of both scene and soil. On the high ground there are outcrops of rock with sandy, acid soils, suitable for heather and bracken. In the valleys the heavy, loamy clay is hard to work but produces rich growth. This is a gentle countryside with nothing harsh about it. It folds you in and makes you feel at home. There are lonely, silent stretches of forest, far from the noise of highways and only disturbed by the 'planes overhead. It is a wonderful setting rich with trees, flowers, birds, animals, butterflies, waterlife and fungi which have all formed part of Peter's life study.

Wildlife can be found inside the church itself. Birds, mostly starlings, find their way into the building through numerous gaps and crannies in the crumbling stone. They are difficult to catch and hard to remove. The other day, during Evening Service, a churchwarden managed to grab a bird that had been dashing itself against the windows and was thrashing away behind one of the pews. He held it firmly, trying to close its beak with his fingers, but it set up such a screaming that the congregation thought he was committing murder and he had to let it go.

For Peter, the church always reminds him of the swifts. "That's a bird that's very hard to photograph" he says, "You can't get near them. They're always in the air. They feed, and court, and even sleep floating on currents of air. They like to nest up under roofs, the higher the better. I often saw them flying in and out of the louvers, the side openings in the tower of the church. So I asked permission of the rector to go up there and see if I could get good pictures of a swift's nest.

"It's quite eerie up there. You have to thread your way through the eight bells so as to get to where the birds fly in. And you have to be sure that the ringers have left the bells hanging down. Because if they were left 'up' on a Saturday morning, for a wedding or such like, you might bring one down by mistake, and you'd go down with it. Luckily the head of the bell-ringers was our postmaster's wife, Mrs Morris, and I'd check with her before I went up. I wouldn't like to be up there if they suddenly started ringing. What with them heavy bells swinging to and fro, and the pretty near deafening sound, you'd be lucky if you come out alive.

"But we got it sorted out and I got pictures of the nest alright. There's not much of it, just the bits of straw and odds and ends they collect on the wing, stuck together with the bird's saliva. They don't lay more than two or three eggs. The parent birds don't come in as regular as many birds, which bring in food every few minutes or so. They have to get insects as they fly. It may take them two or three hours to collect. So the baby swifts have to learn to go a long time without being fed.

"Once some electricians were working up in the belfry, and they came and told me that one of three baby birds in a nest up there was missing. I couldn't go up to look for a couple of days till the next Saturday. When I got there I saw one of the babies fallen out of the nest and laying on the belfry floor. I thought it must be dead, not being fed for so long, but it was only in a kind of stupor. I put it back in with the others, and it was soon as chirpy as the rest, but only half their size. It never caught them up, but it managed to fly away like the others.

"One summer I took a whole party of naturalists up into the tower. We went up soon after eleven o'clock on a Saturday morning. We got all our stands and cameras set up. One of the best naturalists of the whole party had never seen a swift's nest, and he was keen to get a photo. He was leaning right back practically sitting on the big tenor bell. It's a real heavyweight, well over a ton. It's got carved on it 'John Hodson made me 1670'. This is the bell that is struck every hour by a hammer automatically to sound the Church clock. My friend is a bit deaf, especially up in the higher range. In fact, I've made him a hearing aid since, so he can still identify bird-songs and enjoy the dawn chorus. That morning I could hear the click, click of the ratchet drawing back the hammer before it struck. He couldn't. Then it was twelve o'clock. Bong! My friend pretty near jumped out of the belfry. He had just about recovered himself, when Bong! And so it went twelve times. He got the lot. By then he was about driven crazy. 'Don't you ever bring me up here' he said 'before twelve. I'll come just after. I might be able to stand one bang, but that's enough.'

"The ding dong doesn't seem to worry the birds. One year there was a nest built right on the big bell. Those babies must have felt a bit sea-sick at times.

"Swifts are very clever birds. After the parents have fed their young 'uns for about six weeks, they just leave them, take off for Africa most like. They come to us late and leave early. So when the young birds begin to feel hungry and fidget they've got to take off right on their own. No practice flutters, no trial flight. Out of the nest, and that's it. Swifts have such small legs and long wings that they can't settle on the ground and take off again. If you see one on the ground you need to throw it up in the air, and it'll go alright. But for settling, they've got to be up on some high roof or perch. I've never even seen a swift settled on a tree.

"Now they've closed up the louvers with wire netting and the birds can't get in. Too many pigeons about making nuisances of themselves. I've spoken to the rector about it and asked if I could open up a small hole in the netting and put a box in it, specially for the swifts. After all they've got a right to come to Church, same as the rest of us. When I look at swift wings spread out, I wonder sometimes whether the artists who painted angels on our church walls mightn't have got some of their ideas from the swifts.

"You don't have to go far from the centre of the village to start your study of wild life. Why, I've seen a kestrel perched on the base of the cross on top of the church spire. Then right in the village street you get swallows and martins nesting. The swallows like to get indoors in sheds and barns. The martins always nest under the eaves. You can tell a martin from the others by the white patch on its rump. The saying in our parts is that some old saint or bishop Martin got into mischief and was found somewhere where he shouldn't have been. They chased him and caught hold of a bit of his habit and tore it away, showing the white shirt underneath. A more respectable story is that Martin gave half his cloak away to a poor beggar. Anyway the name of the bird martin is supposed to come from the old monk's habit torn at the back. Bats will also roost on the houses under the side tiles and go in under the roofs. I brought my electronic equipment along once to catch them in the dusk as they flew out to get food. But not a single one came out that night. I reckon my electronics must have upset theirs. You know, I'm sure, that bats give out a very high pitched sound too high for humans to hear. It echoes back from any object it meets, so that the bat can steer at high speed and avoid collisions, or else it can locate insects and the like for food.

"I've seen a fox in your garden and I showed you where badgers had got hold of a couple of wasps nests and destroyed them. Then I'm sure you've seen the bodies of hedgehogs run over on the roads. It's easier to see them dead than when they're alive. The hedgehog sleeps mostly in the day and hibernates during winter. It comes out at night to sniff out insects, snails, slugs and worms. It is a tough, courageous animal and will attack rats, frogs and even snakes. The poison of an adder doesn't seem to worry it. It will roll up into a ball and let the snake attack it with its poison again and again. Then when all the venom is used up and the snake is drowsy, the hedgehog will kill it. Talking of snakes, I remember when you had a really big one stretched across your front hall. It was during a hot, parched spell, and the poor creature was desperate for a drink. I expect it seemed a bit scary, especially as you had a baby in the house. But it was only a grass snake and quite harmless.

"If you see a long snake in England, you can be pretty sure that it's harmless. Our only poisonous snake is the adder. An adder is never longer than a couple of feet, and you can tell it by a dark zigzag down its back and what looks like a letter V on its head. You don't need to be afraid of snakes. That flicking tongue of their's darting out and in is not their sting, but their instrument of smell, and their hiss is a way of scaring off enemies. They hunt frogs and fish and are good swimmers. They can dislocate their jaws and swallow a large frog whole. If you have ever touched a snake you'll know they are not wet and slimy, but soft and dry and really quite pleasant. An adder would not attack you unless you were to tread on it by mistake. If you did ever get a bite, you should see a doctor at once. But that is something very rare indeed.

"You may occasionally see a snake skin by the side of a path in the woods. It's often near a patch of heather. Snakes cast off their skin and they probably use the heather to help shrug themselves out of the old one, which they outgrow like an old suit. As it comes off they emerge with a new skin from underneath.

"I'll tell you how I got my picture of an adder. I was walking in the woods with a friend, and there it was right on our path. It was going to slip away fast into the grass verge, before I could get my camera going. But my friend was carrying a small garden chair, to rest his legs bird-watching. He managed to get the four legs of his chair right over the spot where the adder lay, and every time the snake made a dash for cover, he turned his chair so that one of the legs blocked the snake's way. I was waiting for the angry creature to turn on him or, worse still, on me. I was ready with a stick in case. But the snake spit his anger out on the chair leg instead of us. It grabbed the chair, and poured out quite a flood of venom all over it. As soon as the venom was out, the snake became relaxed and sleepy, and the result was that I had a go with my camera, and got a good picture, instead of a very nasty bite.

"But to come back again to your garden. One picture that I'd never been able to get was the lesser spotted woodpecker. And then, that young lady from Australia, who came to stay at your house, found a little bird drowning in an old metal bath-tub down in your paddock, the one used to water the Shetland ponies. It had gone in for a bath, and its wings got too wet to fly, and its claws couldn't grip the side of the tub. Your friend took pity and brought the little bird in and dried it off and warmed it up by an electric fire. She put it for the night in my garden shed, and when I found it next day, I saw at once that it was a lesser spotted, a real find. So I got a picture, before we let it go. By this time it was dried out. It flew to the top of an ash, looked around to find its bearings, let out a short burst of sound and was off. I shall look out for it again. Lesser spotteds like apple trees. You might find them more round a garden than in the woods. Thanks to your friend, we saved a bird, and I got a picture into the bargain. Funny thing it was Friday, the thirteenth.

"Another rare bird in these parts that I found in a garden is the waxwing. This was a Sunday morning when I was still in bed. A fellow down the village started banging on my door, saying that there were a couple of waxwings in his garden. They like to eat berries and, when the winter has been specially severe in Scandinavia, they are apt to come down here. Well I was dressed and on my bike and down in his garden all in ten minutes, and I got some good pictures. They call it waxwing on account of a spot that looks like red sealing wax on its wings. Another bird you may see in your garden is the spotted flycatcher. Like the swallows and swifts it flies over from Africa in May.

"There's an elderly man living in the area, who can't get out much, but he sits at home and watches crows dive-bombing a squirrel's drey, as they call it, built in the fork of an oak tree in his garden. He's never seen them actually hit one but they certainly make the squirrels hop around a bit. Squirrels are graceful creatures, jumping and gliding from branch to branch, until they almost seem to fly. They look pretty enough up on their hind legs as they crack a nut. They'll even feed from your hand. But I've no use for squirrels. They don't only take young birds – they'll gnaw into the bark of trees, and damage, or even destroy them altogether. The red squirrels have practically died out around here. But nothing seems to check the grey ones. The government tried with rewards for shooting them. But the squirrels go on.

"Another animal you may suddenly find right by your own home is a frog. I remember a driveway close here suddenly alive with thousands of small frogs. Frogs are great migrators. Suddenly, they'll go to some pond to mate and lay their eggs that will hatch out into tadpoles in the spring. Once, down on the old railway line, I saw thousands of tiny frogs climbing out of a pool of water that had lain for some weeks during an unusually wet spell. If the sun had come out sooner, the pool would have dried up and the tadpoles all have died. But they got away with it.

"If you keep a bird table, you can sit right at home and study birds all day long, the tits and the robins will make friends with you and hop right into your house.

"The tit is a clever bird. It is usually the great tit that will peck a hole through the top of your milk bottle and suck out the cream, leaving you skim milk. I've been told quite seriously that the tits in some districts will deliberately choose gold rather than silver top bottles. They have learned that it is better quality cream.

"Well, all this, and much more beside, you can see without ever leaving the village, or your own home. But if you want to hear and see more, then you'll have to follow me a bit further round my three-mile patch."

The Stream

THE LITTLE stream that flows east from Rotherfield is the beginning of
the river Rother, but the river did not give its name to the village. It was
the other way round. Back in Roman times the river was called
Lemanus. In 1332, the tax rolls describe a man called "Gilbert atte
Limene" in the township of Mayfield, showing that as late as the four-
teenth century, this, and not "Rother" was the name by which the
stream was known. Its source is a little south of the village and it rises
literally under a big house called Rotherhurst.

When my sister and I were children some of our closest friends, the
Sidey family, lived in this big house with a glorious view across the
Weald to the Downs and the sea. One of our treats was to be invited to
tea and then to be taken down into a dark, eerie cellar where you could
see the river bubbling up under the house. It ran right across the cellar
where it made itself a trough and then disappeared again into the

ground to reappear outside in the garden running down through a rock garden and several pools. It was an amazement to us that this was the very same river that we had seen at Rye, with many a barge or fair-sized sea-going ship sailing up the harbour or anchored to its shore.

The Rother still rises under the house, just under the music room, but it is all blocked in and we do not see the river now until it emerges from a pipe at the bottom of Rotherhurst garden, and then runs down through a series of pools which the local farmer hopes to stock with fish.

For some years now Peter has taken pictures along the banks of the Rother, beginning in spring with the wild daffodils or Lent lilies, kingcups, primroses, lesser celandine, the early purple orchids, which like the damp soil by the stream, the meadow sweet with its lovely scent, and the greater willow herbs, growing five and six feet tall.

One golden autumn afternoon Peter set out specially to photograph sunbeams and I went with him. It was Saint Luke's Little Summer, the spell of warm sunny weather that often comes around October 18, just when you think that winter is upon you. The low autumn sun was shining through the turning trees, some of them still wet with the heavy morning mist and dew. It cast a delicate pattern of sparkle and shadow. The woods along the stream were unearthly quiet. All nature seemed to be still, preparing for the winter days ahead. A jay gave a single sharp cry, as we approached, to warn all and sundry of our arrival. "We call him 'the watchman of the woods'," said Peter. "One cry is enough." Later the alarm note was taken up by a wren. But nothing stirred; nothing until we came to a spot where a sudden burst of song from a robin filled the air with the sheer joy of music.

Peter stopped by a thick holly bush to point out a sleeper's nest, the winter quarters of a dormouse, preparing for a long night. He peered very carefully through the finely woven ball of grass and leaves.

"I wonder if there's anyone at home. No one. See how dry it is in there; and warm. He'll get a good sleep there and won't be disturbed among all them prickles.

"Now, this tidy nest belonged to a blackbird. It's an old one but they're so beautifully made and shaped that they last for years. See the soft layer of moss and leaves the blackbird lays down in his home. Wall-to-wall carpeting, you might say. The thrush leaves his nest with just the bare mud floor. That's how you can tell the difference between the nests. I sometimes tie a small mirror on the end of a long pole, so as to see inside without disturbing anything. That nest looks as good as when it was first built but the birds won't come back to it. Oh, no. They'll want new ones in the spring. Birds seem to love nest building for the joy of doing it. A woodpecker drills a fresh hole every year. You can hear him tap-tapping inside and see the chippings come out. A wren may build several nests but use only one. Maybe their wives are as choosy as ours! They like house-hunting and aren't too easily satisfied.

"I always look out for the first migrant birds of spring. The first one is the chiff-chaff: I found a nest this year with nine young ones. Then comes the blackcap who wastes no time on arrival, makes a nest in less than a week and hatches in ten to twelve days. Then after another ten days or so the young birds are gone. Lovely singer the male blackcap, pours out a whole medley of different sounds and tunes, some of them copied from other birds. It's strange to think of these small birds flying

perhaps thousands of miles to get here, maybe over the Sahara desert from Africa. The female is still called blackcap, but her cap is brown. Then there's the redstart, with its handsome white cap, black collar, chestnut breast and tail. It loves to show off its bright red tail when it's courting and chasing its lady love from bough to bough. It makes its nest in holes in dead trees. It's a great mistake to clear away dead trees from a wood. They are the home of many birds and the mass of insects that feed them. There are plenty of other birds to be seen around here, especially the tits, the marsh tit, the blue tit and the great tit.

"The most exciting bird to photograph is the kingfisher. To get that famous flash of blue, you've got to be at the right place at the right time, ready to fire your camera to catch a bird flying in at forty miles an hour with a fish in its beak.

"I'll show you my home-made apparatus sometime if you like, though it will take some explaining! Me and a couple of mates have experimented with all sorts of equipment over five or six years. We've used the base of an ordinary windscreen wiper to fire the camera. We plug this into the camera with a longish cable release. Then to break the beam as the bird flies past, we've used a small automatic fire alarm, only we reverse the bias, so that whereas in the fire alarm it is light that sets off the alarm, with us it is the breaking off of the light by the bird flying past, that sets off the mechanism.

"There is a very slight delay between the breaking of the beam and the firing of the camera, so as to get the bird right in your frame. But they can't get away from us. It's the cheap way out and it works. It's not cost us more than a few pounds, and it's easy to operate.

"Where do I get my best pictures of kingfishers? Ah, now you're asking. I don't tell too much about the where's and when's. You'll get sightseers trampling down your hides, scaring the birds or animals away. I'll take proper nature-lovers with me if they'll make themselves not too much seen or heard, and promise not to tell half the village.

"If you want to take pictures of kingfishers, it's best to be out early in the morning. Round about six o'clock is usually the best time when the young birds are hungriest. The nest is tunnelled in the river bank. It goes in as deep as two or three feet. The tunnel slopes upward so that after the birds have eaten a fish, the slime will run out. Usually at the top the tunnel turns so that the round white eggs don't roll out too. Five, six or seven eggs are the usual number. You set up your camera trained on the mouth of the tunnel. I use flash with the camera shut down. Then you wait.

"With luck it may not be more than twenty or thirty minutes. Then you may have the good fortune to see the parent bird fly in, with a fish in its beak. He'll settle on a nearby branch and kill or stun the fish by hitting it hard on either side on wood. Then you may see a delicate operation when the bird turns the fish completely round in its beak. This is so it can take it to its young head-first. Without that, the birds would choke on the fins. Each of the young birds may be lucky enough to get a whole fish to digest.

"They'll eat whatever is going. Minnows probably or sticklebacks, or it may be a water beetle. Whatever it is it will keep the feeders happy for a while, so it may be a long time before the parent bird is back. You will probably get only one chance for your picture. When I'm giving my picture shows, I show a picture of the kingfisher entering the nest. Then I tell the audience to blink and look at the same picture again, and I tell them that that's the picture of the bird coming out of the nest. You see it comes out just exactly the way it goes in. The same picture does for both. The only difference is when it's coming out it hasn't got a fish in its beak – but in this picture you don't see the beak. That's hidden.

"There's one picture, though, that I'm still trying to get. That is when the parent bird (it can be male or female), soon as it's fed its young, it dives straight back into the water to wash itself. It will always turn and drop instantly. The thing is to know ahead of time just exactly where that's going to be.

"There are many fewer kingfishers around here than there used to be. In that very hard winter of 1962–3 every bit of water froze over for

weeks on end and many of the birds starved to death. Since then they began coming back, but lately again they've been disappearing. There weren't any at all last year.

"I think the minks get them. It was a bad thing for our wild life, when they imported minks from America. The idea was to grow them in special mink farms for the valuable fur. But then you see they escape, and pretty soon you find them all over the place. During the big floods a few years ago, the rain flooded a mink farm nearby and the mink cages started floating downstream. Of course the animals escaped and there's no holding them now. Most destructive creatures they are. They can swim like anything, and they'll eat practically anything in sight. They'll raid islands that are sanctuaries for wild life. Like foxes they'll kill even when they aren't hungry. They are upsetting the whole balance of nature. You'd think it would be worth catching them for their skins but unfortunately the wild mink don't have commercial value. Their colours won't match and the quality isn't good enough."

We had walked further down to where the stream widened. Here we sat on some rocks to enjoy the sunshine. These woods at one time belonged to a country club and here we could see the stone ledges and small waterfalls which had been made as trout runs. The stone face was deliberately left rugged and uneven so the trout could flip up and over, as they fought their way upstream to spawn. There were pools made for fishing and even the relic of an old diving board invited a quiet swim. But now the stream is silted with mud.

"This is where I've taken some of my winter, spring and summer pictures. I show the same stretch as it is on an icy January day, and then the very same place in May, or again in July.

"There are so many things to photograph. There are the moorhens, of course. You've seen them around the little pond at the bottom of your garden. We might put up a hide and see if we can get some good pictures. You must hear them often enough. It's a harsh kind of croak, or cluck. They are shy birds and not good flyers. They'll often sit under the water with only the very tip of their beak showing, or you can track them as they swim by a row of bubbles.

"Then there are the wagtails. We have what is called the grey wagtail, though it is really a handsome yellow underneath. Its back is grey touched with blue. Its long black tail is as long as the rest of it. It is with us all winter, and likes to nest near waterfalls, like this one here.

"In the stream itself besides the odd trout, there are the tiddlers like minnows and sticklebacks. A bit bigger is the bullhead, hiding away under hollow stones or in thick mud or weeds. It may come out to feed and you can spot it. The water voles are scarcer now, thanks to the minks, but you may see them sitting by the water bank nibbling the heads of plants, then diving into the water for a swim. Or throw a bit of apple core into the stream and they may come up for a bite. They are equally at home in the water or on land. They have their nests on shore, but the entrance may be under the surface of the water.

"Of course there's a great world of smaller creatures on the surface, or under the water, but you really need a microscope more than a camera to make a proper study of it all. You must know the water boatman – it's also called the backswimmer because it often swims upside-down. It 'rows' through the water with long back legs looking like a couple of oars. It has a poisonous bite and does attack tadpoles and small fish. The pond-skater sculls about on the surface of the water with long middle legs. It can submerge itself carrying down a supply of air trapped by its body hairs. Some water bugs operate under water with a kind of snorkel arrangement attached to the body and sticking up above the surface. They must have a regulator inside that stops them going too deep and drowning themselves. Another insect you may see is the damsel fly. It has a nice name and a pretty blue colour, but it is the enemy of lesser bugs.

"A river bank is a good place for wild flowers. Some of them are two or three feet tall, like the yellow flag. Then you get snowdrops of course and the water variety of the mint that cooks love. Some of these flowers come down the streams from gardens and establish themselves where it's damp and they are most at home.

"In that quiet pool you'll find the wild water lily. It is quite small, not like the larger water lilies that are garden grown. As a gardener I had to lower boxes of these garden lilies into a pond and then bring them up again for renewal. We call the wild lily the brandy bottle. It smells a bit like brandy and its centre can look like a green bottle.

"Talking of scents, in the spring you might notice an oniony smell. That comes from the wild garlic, or ramsons. Walk around them and you'd better take a bath when you get home. If the cows get too much of them, it will affect the taste of the cream and butter. Of course the banks of the stream are full of primroses in spring. Rotherfield was famous at one time for its cowslips. There aren't so many now. You do get a hybrid around here, primrose and cowslip mixed. No, it's not an oxlip, but a real hybrid. You'll find whole masses of golden yellow kingcups. Marsh marigold is another name for them. Another nice flower around the stream is the balsam. We call it policeman's helmet, because of the shape of its purple flower, it's like the old fashioned bobby's helmet, or the fireman's helmet of today.

"But as well as the plants and animals there's the water itself with all its reflections. It is an artist's paradise. Look there! What do you think of those sunbeams shining over the water through grass and leaves? That wooden post helps to focus the picture all right. I think we might have a go."

Nature at Night

IN PETER'S early logging days, when evening came and work was over, the older ones might make off to some nearby local, and Peter and his next older brother would sit by the fire, while the embers died away, and listen to the hoot of the owl, as nature's night life began.

"Ever since those early days," said Peter, "there's nothing I've enjoyed more than setting out on the old bike just as it's getting dusk, and spending some hours out in the country at night. At first it was mostly poaching. Later on it was a case of staying quiet and listening. To begin with you're apt to think there's nothing to hear, nothing except a dog barking on a distant farm. Nature beds down quietly and neatly and doesn't make a fuss of it. But bit by bit you become aware of the sounds around you. When I was younger, the air would be alive with crickets, rubbing and rasping their legs and wings. I don't hear them now, but that's not because they aren't there. When you're older your range of hearing gets less and the high-pitched sounds don't register any more. Then you may pick up a sound a bit like the cricket, but it comes from a bird, the grasshopper warbler. We haven't had them around lately since the pine trees have grown higher. They can't get in to nest. But we had a fire down near the railway line some years ago. It burnt off a big piece of forest land, and now they've replanted with new baby trees. We ought to be getting the grasshopper warbler back, and I'll be going down there around ten o'clock in the summer, when it's just dark, to see if I can hear them. I think I can still get the pitch of this sound, though my friend who goes with me can't. After that, around eleven, it will be glow worm time and I may get some pictures of them.

"As the moon comes up under the trees, and your eyes get used to the light, you may see a badger shining like a silver skeleton, or a deer silhouetted against the sky. Or there's a nightjar sitting on a post maybe churring away. If you try a photograph by flash its great big eyes will come out like an aeroplane with two headlights. There are hedgehogs around snuffling for food and moles bury underground. You won't see them, unless you set traps like my brother did.

"The woods can seem full of ghosts, a branch of dead wood, fluffy and white, can appear almost human, or a holly tree look like a big horse heading straight towards you. In the winter the screaming yowl of a vixen in the mating season, mixed with the sharp *'yap, yap'* of a courting male can send a shiver down your back. Add to that, it's easy to get lost in a wood at night, especially when there's a bit of low mist, and you can't seen the breaks in the trees. All you've got is the hoot of an owl to keep you company.

"People think that the call of the owl is *'tuwhit a woo'*. But it takes two birds to make the *'tuwhit a woo'* sound. It's a duet. The long drawn out *'Woo'* or *'Twoo'* is probably the male, and his mate replies with a sharp *'twit'* or *'kwick'*.

"My old dad used to like to tell a story of some fellow coming home to his place in the woods late at night, perhaps after a few too many at the pub. This fellow got lost among the trees and, in panic, he started yelling for help, 'Man lost. Man lost.' In reply came an eerie sound *'whoo, whoo'*. 'Fred so-and-so from Frant' came the nervous reply. I don't know if the owl got him home that night!

"The commonest owl in our parts is the tawny or brown owl. They are not easy to photograph, because, of course, it is night when they fly to the nest, and their flight is completely silent. You can't hear them coming in the dark. But I've got some good pictures of owls, including one of a mother bird feeding her young. Of course, first of all I had to find the nest. Owls may nest in a hollow tree or a hole in a bank or even among branches on the ground. I found a nest a year or two ago right near the bottom of your garden.

"Well, this particular nest was quite high up in a tree, and there were eggs in it. The owl will lay its eggs separately with a few days in between. The number of eggs it lays will depend on the supply of food. If there's plenty of food around, the female may lay three or four. Well, I photographed the nest and the eggs. Then I put up a small hide of hessian on a bank opposite at the same height as the nest. Then when the eggs hatched out, and the young'uns were there, I set up my camera and got it all focused and ready. I'd do this a couple of hours before dark. Then there would be another hour or two to wait in the hide, before the female would fly in with food. The difficulty is to know when she's coming. You can't see her in the dark, and you can't hear her, even as she's flying right over the hide. You can sometimes get a hint that she's coming, because the young birds in the nest get excited and you hear them. Then I noticed that the only thing you could hear was a slight thump as the mother landed by the nest. It would rattle like a drum. It took many nights of waiting and watching before I got the hang of how to get the picture. I'd go out to the hide every third night or so, and wait. It was still often frosty at night and the hide was cramped. No room to take food and too noisy to eat. I'd get as watchful and impatient as those young owls in the nest.

"Then at last one night it all came right. I heard the squeak and excitement of the young'uns in the nest. Then not a sound as the female flew silently right over the hide, 'til I heard the sudden beat of the bird landing, and I fired my camera which set off the flash. There's some pictures give me more pleasure than all the rest and this is one. I don't say it's my best or prettiest, but I had to plan and work hard for it, and then the bird's sound and the camera's flash just came together. Perfect! There's a special thrill when that happens.

"To get back to the owls, this female brought mice, moles, beetles and all that. But tawny owls bring small birds also or young ones. It is always the female who brings in the food. The male stays some distance away. He probably collects the food and feeds the female, who takes it to the nest.

"After I had been watching the owl nest for a few weeks, I noticed one of the baby owls had fallen out of the nest into a tiny stream. It had managed to scramble up on to a piece of floating wood, and there it was slowly floating downstream. I had to rescue it of course and I put it somewhere safe, while I fetched a ladder so as to get it back into its nest. I had to walk half a mile or so to fetch a fair size ladder from a garden where I worked. I climbed up and put the little bird back in its nest. Otherwise a fox or some other animal would have got it for certain. I returned the ladder, but by the time I got back to the nest, there was the young rascal out again. So back I go once more and fetch back my ladder. This time I brought some nails and a hammer. So after I'd put the young'un back again, I made a little wooden fence at the edge of the nest to keep the family in, and to safeguard the babies when they make a rush forward for food. When the baby owls get a bit bigger, they leave the nest and, using their claws, scramble up and down along the branches, for all the world like little monkeys.

"You have to make a nightwatch to study owls. You'll rarely see a tawny owl by day, unless it's disturbed sleeping. Then if it flies the other smaller birds will mob it; blackbirds, tits, finches and the like swooping down and around it, regular dive-bombing.

"An owl is a bird of prey isn't it? The smaller birds buzz it, to scare it off. I have known naturalists put up a stuffed owl somewhere, so as to get pictures of the birds around it. I don't go in for that kind of thing. I've noticed though that when the female flies in with a bird in its powerful claws, she always crushes the bird's head with her beak before she feeds it to its young. Some people I know have kept a tame owl for the past fourteen years. As a matter of fact it isn't legal to keep an owl, or any wild bird taken from the nest, unless you have a licence which can be very hard to come by. This owl was injured and so badly damaged that it still can't fly. The lady who keeps it has bred her own mice to feed it. She's bought it meat at the butcher's. Children will bring it along a dead bird. I notice, even though the bird's dead, Olley the owl (we call it Olley after the naturalist Olley Kite) will always crush the bird's head with its beak. Olley's another tawny owl, but there are other owls out at night.

"I got a nice picture of a barn owl, right at eye level, face to face. That was in the early days. I haven't seen a barn owl around Rotherfield since 1963. This one was nesting in a dovecot over the garage at Holme Park, one of the big houses. The barn owl does not build a nest. It will lay its white eggs in a corner of a barn loft, or a church roof.

"To get the pictures of the barn owl, I got up into the attic over the garage, and then opened the trap door up into the dovecot. There was just room to get my head through, and I had an awful job pushing my camera and flash through ahead of me. As soon as I was up there, the mother who was sitting up on a beam flew out, and the young ones, they'd be about a month old I suppose, immediately pretended to be dead. They fell limp on the floor, and did not move a feather even when I picked one up. The minute I put my torch out and waited in the dark they started sqeaking and moving again.

"I got another nice close up of an adult barn owl out in the woods. It was an odd male, I suppose. Probably not mated up. You can see a small speck of blood on its breast, where it had been carrying a mouse or something it had caught.

"As I've told you, in these first days of taking pictures, pretty well all my gadgets were home-made. We may have invented some of them for all I know. I made a brass piston to fire the camera, and an old motor horn bulb or a bulb from my wife's scent bottle to work the piston. I could set up my flash about four foot from the bird, and then work the camera through a tube from about twenty-five to thirty feet away. A close-up look at a barn owl is an eerie sight, a big round white face with huge, staring black eyes. Combine that with its long-drawn-out screech, and you can believe in ghosts all right.

"The barn owls seem to have disappeared now, along with some other birds, after that bad winter of '63–'64, there's no sign of them. We got steady frost and snow right from Boxing day to pretty near Easter. The trees were covered with freezing spray. Birds got frozen in. There were woodpeckers I saw frozen into their holes.

"There's another owl that I've only seen once around Rotherfield. That's the so-called long-eared owl. Its cry is a haunting sound, more like a moan than a screech. The long tufted 'ears' that give this owl its name are not ears really, only plumes on its head. Its true ears are very keen. Like most owls, it can see and hear very sharply, and can pounce on mice or voles or young birds like lightning. This is another species that seems to have disappeared altogether around Rotherfield. It might

come back as the new conifers grow taller and thicker. Owls like dark secluded places where they can hide up all day. But there's one owl, the little owl, comes out in the day time. You might see it sitting on a post if you are lucky. It is sometimes called the French owl. I believe it comes from France, and either migrated or was brought over.

"The nightjar arrives from Africa, Ethiopia I think. It comes late, well into May, and is mated up before it arrives. It doesn't make a nest. It just lays its two eggs on the ground, and relies for its protection on its amazing powers of camouflage. You can almost walk over a nightjar and not see it, as its feathers blend into the colour of branches or dead leaves. Once you've found a nightjar's 'scrape', you have to make careful plans if you want to get photos. First I put up a piece of wood close to the spot, big enough for the bird to perch on. Then I make a hide quite a way away, then I move the hide carefully nearer and nearer. You can move it a little every two hours, until you get within about twelve feet. The female bird will sit tight. By staying still, its scent disappears and even a fox will pass close by without noticing it; though a fox can hear the squeak of the babies in the eggs before they are hatched. The male will come and perch on the post several times in the night churring away just to let his missus know he's there. After the eggs were hatched I'd go to the hide nearly every night, I'd get pictures of the open beaks waiting for food. Also I've caught both the male and the female sitting on the stump. The grown birds have very big wings. You will notice the stiff hairs on either side of the beak. When she comes to her young with a big mouthful of moths and such, these hairs prevent the food flying away out of the sides and drives it forward straight into the hungry mouths of her family.

"People used to call nightjars 'goat-suckers'. There was an old superstition that nightjars actually fed on goat's milk, milking direct. The goats were supposed to die as a result. It's all wrong, of course.

"Gilbert White, the eighteenth-century naturalist, has a lot to say about nightjars. He spent hours watching them and listening to the churring sound that the male makes. I've been given quite a lot of nature books and I look up things in Gilbert White. He describes how a

Rotherfield village from the top of Argos Hill windmill.

Village and farm

Opposite top left: A swift (*Apus apus*) flies in through a small opening to feed its young in its nest in the bell tower of Rotherfield church.

Opposite bottom left: A great tit (*Parus major*) in Peter's garden. One of the most noisy and hungry of birds, its chicks devour thousands of caterpillars during the few weeks that they are in the nest.

Opposite right: A mistle thrush (*Turdus viscivorus*) nesting in the strod, or fork, of an apple tree.

Left: A wren (*Troglodytes troglodytes*) nesting in a windbreak in a woodcutter's shed. The male makes several nests and the female selects the one she likes best.

Below: A pied wagtail (*Motacilla alba yarellii*) which built its nest in the same woodcutter's shed.

Above: The white admiral (*Ladoga camilla*), now rare around Rotherfield.
Above right: The painted lady (*Cynthia cardui*) a Mediterranean migrant.
Below: The red admiral (*Vanessa atalanta*) is also a migrant.
Below right: The small tortoiseshell (*Aglais urticae*) hibernates in Britain.
Far right: The peacock butterfly (*Inachis io*) also hibernates.

Above: The spiked rampion (*Phyteuma orbiculare*), a very rare flower, possibly to be found only in Sussex, is carefully protected.
Above right: The common spotted orchid (*Dactylorhiza fuchsii*).
Top right: Rotherfield was once famous for its cowslips (*Primula veris*).
Bottom right: Field bindweed (*Convolvulus arvensis*) on a wall.
Opposite top left: The primrose (*Primula vulgaris*), harbinger of spring.
Opposite bottom left: The blue sow thistle (*Cicerbita macrophylla*), rare in this area.
Opposite right: Goatsbeard (*Tragopogon pratensis*). The seed heads are blown, like those of dandelions, to tell the time of day. The flowers close up around noon: hence the popular name 'Jack-go-to-bed-at-noon'.

Far left: Teasel (*Dipsacus fullonum*) makes an attractive winter decoration for the house. Its heads were used for teasing wool. Goldfinches feed on its seeds.
Left: Grass vetchling (*Lathurus nissolia*) the only peaflower with grasslike leaves.

The stream

Below: A blue damselfly (*Coenagrion puella*). Related to the dragonfly, but smaller, damselflies are found over the water of streams and ponds.
Right: Ramsons (*Allium ursinum*) and bluebells (*Endymion non-scriptus*) line a bridle-path crossing the River Rother. The ramsons has a strong smell of garlic.

Left: The Rother in winter, with trout leaps in the distance.
Above: A female great spotted woodpecker (*Dendrocopus major*).
Opposite top left: Balsam (*Impatiens glandulifera*). Its seed pods burst at the slightest touch, earning it the name of 'Jumping Jack'.
Opposite bottom left: The fertile spike of a horsetail (*Equisetum telmateia*).
Opposite top right: A yellow water lily (*Nuphar lutea*), sometimes called 'brandy bottle' because its flowers smell like stale brandy, and fruits resemble flasks.
Opposite bottom right: Kingcups (*Caltha palustris*), or marsh marigolds, grow where the water is still.

Left: A kingfisher (*Alcedo atthis*), a fish in its mouth, perches for a moment before going into its nest to feed its young.
Above: A robin (*Erithacus rubecula*) in flight, leaving the bird table. A stop-action picture taken with home-made equipment.
Right: A pair of grey wagtails (*Motacilla cinerea*), both male and female feeding their young in a nest on an old iron bridge.

Nature at night

Left: A barn owl (*Tyto alba*) leaving its nest in a hole in a tree. It is a ghostly bird in sound and shape. Pesticides have helped to make this a rare bird in our parts.

Below: This baby tawny owl (*Strix aluco*) fell from its nest into a small stream but managed to scramble on to a piece of floating wood from which it was rescued by Peter.

Right: After this accident had been repeated Peter fixed a 'gate' across the nest.

nightjar, or churn-owl, as he is sometimes called, settled on a small straw hut, where he and his friends were drinking tea, and how the vibrations of its tiny throat set the whole building reverberating.

"Sometimes it sounds like the croaking of a frog but usually it is just a monotonous vibration. The nightjar can also clap its wings so that it sounds just like the crack of a whip. The sound could be a mating call, I suppose. But I think it's a warning, like, to other birds. 'This is my territory! Get out! Keep out!'

"Another bird that you can hear at night is the woodcock. It gives a deep throated croak as it flies back and forth marking out its territory, methodical like. This is known as roding. Somewhere hidden in the area is the nest right on the ground. You might put up a female if you're lucky (he may have two or three mates). But a woodcock will stay right where it is if you're looking for it. Its camouflage is so good.

"Did I ever tell you how I was out one day in the woods looking for a woodcock to photograph? It's so well camouflaged that it's very hard to spot. It's practically got eyes at the back of its head, but it'll sit tight on its eggs till the very last minute, if it sees you coming. Well, I'd been tramping back and forth hoping to spot a sitting bird, when I met a fellow with a dog. We stopped and chatted a while and I asked him if he'd seen a woodcock.

"'Not a sign' he said. We talked on and then suddenly his dog made a dash right through my legs and a woodcock got up within a yard of where we were standing. It had been sitting there the whole time, and neither of us spotted it.

"If you want to get a picture of the woodcock's chicks you need to look slippy, as they leave the nest only a few hours after they are hatched. The woodcock feeds at night, and uses its long beak to dig into soft ground for worms.

"As your eyes get used to the dark, you will see more and more. You may get a glimpse of a moth in the moonlight. The elephant hawk moth is one of the big ones, and you might spot it at dusk as it lays its eggs on willowherb. I've seen and photographed a death's head hawk moth, the largest moth we have in Britain. But this was in the day, and it wasn't a

The tawny owls' mother returns bringing food for her brood.

very good specimen. Some people spread a mixture of beer and treacle on trees, and then go out and catch or photograph moths as they sit there and guzzle, getting drunk. I don't go in for that. I do collect some of the caterpillars, bring them home and rear them. They lie in cocoons or chrysalises during the winter and then, when they hatch out in spring, I photograph them as soon as they have dried out, and then I let them go. You get perfect specimens that way. Moths can't bring their wings up together as butterflies do. There's another easy way to tell a moth from a butterfly; the moth does not have the little knobs at the end of its antennae. A moth's life is pretty short. It hatches out, feeds, lays its eggs and dies.

"Then there's glow-worms of course. Neither the male nor female are rightly speaking worms. They are beetles, although the female is a caterpillar-like creature, a little like a woodlouse. She can climb up a plant, and will twist her body from side to side displaying a luminous light on her backside. This is to attract the male, which is more obviously like a beetle and can fly. The male can glow very faintly too. I counted thirty-eight glow-worms on one length of path in the pine woods, during the hot summer a couple of years ago. They feed on tiny snails. I thought that was a record, but only the other night I took some ladies out to see the glow-worms and they counted ninety-six in the same stretch. A good year for snails is a good year for glow-worms.

"So the night goes on, and as nature sleeps, you begin to feel a bit sleepy yourself. There have been times when, coming home from a spell of badger watching sometime after midnight, I've rattled a fence as I climbed over it, and suddenly a nightingale has burst into song. I remember when our woods were full of nightingales. I had them one year nesting in the long grass both sides of our cottage. Did you ever hear about that lady in Surrey who used to take her 'cello out at night, and, as she played, she'd set the nightingales singing as well? I don't know if it was love of music set them going, or if the lady with the 'cello was just keeping them awake. Nightingales sing in the daytime too, but when they have it all to themselves at night, they make a lovely solo. I've heard one singing, and got up in the night, walked nearly a mile to record the sound and then heard Mayfield Church chime four. They haven't been around here now for several years, but someone told me not so long ago that he and two friends had heard one in these parts again. I haven't yet. My ears and eyes are open.

"I was mentioning Gilbert White. There's a poem he wrote in his book about nature at night. I like it, and it fits in with so many things that I've heard and seen myself. Do you know it?"

When day declining sheds a milder gleam
What time the may-fly haunts the pool or stream;
When the still owl skims round the grassy mead,
What time the timorous hare limps forth to feed;
Then be the time to steal adown the vale,
And listen to the vagrant cuckoo's tale;
To hear the clamorous curlew call his mate,
Or the soft quail his tender pain relate;
To see the swallow sweep the dark'ning plain
Belated, to support her infant train;
To mark the swift in rapid giddy ring
Dash round the steeple, unsubdu'd of wing.

While o'er the cliff th'awakened churn-owl hung
Through the still gloom protracts his chattering song;
While high in air, and poised upon his wings,
Unseen, the soft enamoured woodlark sings;
These, Nature's works the curious mind employ,
Inspire a soothing melancholy joy:
As fancy warms, a pleasing kind of pain
Steals o'er the cheek, and thrills the creeping vein!
Each rural sight, each sound, each small combine;
The tinkling sheep-bell, or the breath of kine;
The new-mown hay that scents the swelling breeze,
Or cottage-chimney smoking through the trees.

The chilling night-dews fall; away, retire;
For see the glow-worm lights her amorous fire.

The Rotherfield Badgers

IT WAS a warm, still evening in July at the height of the hot summer of 1976. Earlier it had looked like rain but, as so often in that particular year, the clouds had scattered leaving the land as parched as before. We had been able to have a barbecue in the garden, over a dozen family and friends, three generations of us. Peter was there, of course, and he helped us to get the charcoal going and grill hamburgers and chicken. Then, as there was time to spend before the big excitement of the evening, we all went indoors to see some of Peter's slides.

But the evening's main event was still to come. As the sky darkened from blue to indigo we set off with Peter and five of the children to try to get a sight of the Rotherfield badgers. It is a short drive to Millhole Wood. This part of the country is now a private reserve belonging to a timber company but people can obtain a key by paying a subscription to a woodland society and members are invited to ride or walk along the paths and firebreaks between the timber. Peter has been made an honorary member and he produced his key.

Soon we were trailing, silent and in single file like a troop of boy-scout trackers, through rough uneven wood and meadowland. The evening bird chorus was over and there was not a sound except for the occasional hoot of an owl just getting up, the flutter of a woodcock doing his roding, or a magpie, homeward bound, after a late evening out on the tiles. The rattle of a stone underfoot or the breaking of a twig brought a "shushing" and looks of disapproval from the rest of the party until, after a mile or so, we arrived at a small clearing in the wood that was banked on one side by tree trunks and big mounds of piled-up earth. It was like a theatre with an apron stage and, tingling with anticipation, our small audience found each their special stall, lying full length on their fronts with eyes focused upon the one or two black

69

openings in the earth that we hoped would be the entrances at which the actors of the evening might appear.

It grew darker and darker, and still there was not a sound, not a sign. There was a longish drive home to Robertsbridge for the children, but still no one moved or gave up. Then it happened. Framed for just a moment in one of the stage entrances was a ripple of white, marked by two streaks of black. Then it was gone. A minute or two later, there it was again. This time the striped mask remained longer, until very slowly and cautiously, it moved towards us. Then we realised that what seemed a rather small head was followed by a surprisingly big body. The whole effect was eerie. We were looking at a large, powerful creature. Its main colouring was dark but, as our eyes grew accustomed to the dim light, and as the animal moved or turned, glimpses of white would come and go.

We lay there quite still and spellbound. Then there was the faintest rustle. Had someone moved? The ghost-like creature turned and disappeared down its dark exit. We were afraid that the performance was prematurely over. But no, the badger had gone to tell the rest of the cast that all was clear.

Very soon there were three, then four, then five of these somewhat clumsy, but surprisingly fast-moving creatures in full view. They were scratching and cleaning themselves and one another with fastidious care, sometimes playing and romping about. But there was more serious business. Peter had invited us to bring along some packets of unsalted peanuts, and with these he had laid out careful tracks leading from near the set to the different places at which we were positioned. These were quickly discovered. Some had been buried as deep as nine inches in the earth, but the badgers quickly smelt them and dug them up. The badgers' sense of smell is much sharper than their sight but such breeze as there was was blowing towards us from where the badgers were, and soon they seemed completely used to the presence of visitors. We could hear the crunch and munch of the peanuts.

Then began the most fascinating scene of all. Very gradually, following the peanut trail, the badgers came nearer to us as we stretched out a flat, open hand well covered with nuts. It was a kind of stately dance, as each animal advanced, retreated, turned and approached again, appetite and shyness, desire and timidity in conflict with each other. Gradually peanuts overcame prudence. An enthralled and excited small boy did not move a muscle as a phantom, which seemed as big as himself, paused and crouched only an inch from his hand. The striped face and grey silvery body were iridescent in the dim light. You wondered who was going to lose nerve and break first, badger or boy. Both held on. And then there came a thrilling moment, when the badger came on the final inch, placed a paw on the boy's hand as though to hold it steady and stop it running away, and with a gentle snuffle ate up two or three peanuts, crunching them in its sharp teeth before backing away. Soon we were all feeding badgers. Fear had gone on both sides. Our peanuts were accepted and so were we.

It was not until some twenty minutes, and our peanuts were gone, that the strange fantasy was over. As mysteriously as they had come, the badgers ambled off in different directions, going in search of further food, or to follow the quite clearly marked badger tracks that over the years their forebears had made for them, leading out to carefully prepared dungpits (for badgers are the cleanest and neatest of animals). They roam over a two mile area which they regard as their own, leaving scent signals as they go to warn other badgers to keep away, but they come back home practically every night.

Our stage lay silent and empty, like any stage, still and bare after the performance. Slowly we left the darkened theatre, savouring what we had seen, almost wondering whether it had really happened, or had been some kind of trick. But it had happened. Our hands, still sticky, were the proof. After the strain of the long silence the children laughed, joked and danced their way back to the car. But we still felt a sense of awe and wonder. Watching the badgers of Rotherfield had been an experience to remember.

Very gradually Peter has yielded some of the story of the Rotherfield badgers. He is never one to talk too freely unless he is sure that you really want to know. And he is afraid of a private and personal experience becoming a tourist attraction. He is always ready to take a friend who is a genuine nature lover on a private expedition to the set, but then in time, friends take friends, others go out exploring on their own, and what took years to build could be destroyed. "Last year," he said, "there were scarcely any badgers. The long drought the year before may have had something to do with it; but it also may have been because insensitive visitors have taken liberties. If you ever want to watch badgers, you have got to be patient. Start a good long way from the set and stay very still. Gradually they may come to accept you, and you can move nearer.

"We've made friends with the badgers but we've never wanted to tame them too much. If they come to trust humans too much, someone might take advantage, try and catch one, or club one to death or use a gun. There's deliberate badger-baiting goes on in some parts of the country, pitting badgers to fight dogs and the like. But our badgers trust us you see. The young ones take us for granted like part of the scenery. I suppose they think our peanuts fall from trees. You can catch a very young badger and tame it at home or in a cage for a year or so. But this is illegal since the recent Badger Act. No, we don't aim to tame badgers like that. They are free to come and go, accept us or leave us, just as they please. We don't take them into our environment. We visit them in theirs.

"Badgers can be brave fighters but I only know one case of anyone being attacked. This fellow got to teasing them with the food, suddenly drawing his hand back and the like. Durned near got his finger bit right off. Serve him damn right. Badgers belong to the weasel family, with their teeth interlocking like. If they really got hold of you, you'd know it. Be sure, if you ever try to feed a badger, to keep your hand flat on the ground and very still.

"Round the neck and shoulders they are very strong. If they are attacked they'll fight back. They could see off any kind of dog, if it came to a fight, I reckon.

"I grew up with badgers, I suppose, living in the woods. I remember back in my poaching days, being out with my brother at night after rabbits and the like. It was a bright moonlight night. Suddenly three badgers come out of the shadows. The moon was behind me, and the three of them together all shimmery in the light looked like a skeleton. I'll tell you I was proper scared; nearly ran.

"Then later, some years after the war, there was a friend of mine. We used to mend old people's wireless sets in the winter for a hobby. Then when the spring came, this fellow (I'll call him Fred. We call everyone Fred, even a badger) he got keen on photography. He'd ask me to go out with him nights trying to photograph fox cubs. He had an old motorbike and I'd ride on the back. It was then we come across badgers. At first we'd watch just for the sake of watching. We took such a liking to them, we became badger-men after that. We got an old army torch from Woolworth, with red and green filters. We always used the red to start with. Then one night we forgot to bring the red, so we used white. Very bright it was. To our surprise the badgers didn't seem to mind a bit. They were getting used to us by then. Fred tried black and white photography with a flash bulb on top of his camera. But he couldn't get near enough for a good shot. So between us we designed some kind of remote control affair. Then we wanted to try cine. We needed more light then, so we brought a generator. The badgers didn't like the noise, chug, chug, chug, and they'd disappear for a while. Then we tried a longer line with the generator back on a land-rover quite a long way away. With the long line the voltage dropped and that didn't work. Then a friend who ran a garage lent us a tractor battery. We'd bring it up to the site in a wheel-barrow. We used car lights and reflectors, and we could swivel them around where we wanted. We could get five minutes or so real good light and we started getting good pictures, didn't seem to worry the badgers. Later on one fellow brought an extra big flash bulb. It went off like a gun. We never saw a badger for a fortnight after that. We didn't ever invite that fellow again. I remember a big white moth attracted to the light, and for quite a long time we saw one of the badgers playing around, trying to catch it, waving its paws in the air, up on its hind legs and all. It never caught it. They are rather clumsy creatures really. They couldn't creep up to anything. They can't catch anything that's moving fast. They like their dinner to be sitting there waiting.

"I've seen them dig out a wasp's nest. They'll dig for young rabbits underground. Every sort of grubs, worms, caterpillars, nuts, acorns, beetles, spiders seem to be what they eat most. They love blackberries in season, or anything sweet. They are sometimes accused of killing young sheep, but I've not seen traces of it. If it does happen it's pretty rare, or perhaps they find one dead already. They'll eat high, rare meat if they can get it. They'll eat voles and mice of course, and in that they are really the farmer's friend. No one attacks them. Pretty well their only enemy is man.

"Down in the West Country I'm told they've been gassing and killing off badgers wholesale. They say they give the cattle TB. They reckon if they root it out there altogether, they'll stop it spreading to other parts. And they reckon that a new lot of clean, healthy badgers will come back eventually. Mind you, what I say is it was probably the cattle give the poor old badger the TB in the first place. Besides, when they put poison gas down there, what else are they killing?

"They hadn't better try it on my badgers. I've been watching them for twenty years and more. Not many were photographing or taming badgers then. There are plenty now. We had all kinds of fun and adventures in them days, before anyone knew of our badgers but us. I remember one night Fred was moving around quite close to the set, trying to get photographs. Suddenly he slipped and fell clean into one of the set entrances. Made a hell of a racket. Two frightened badgers made straight for the same hole and scrambled and tore their way right over Fred trying to get back to shelter. I don't know who was most scared, the badgers or Fred. Another night, Fred said 'I think I'll go round the other side of the set, see what I can see there'.

"Badger sets are quite big. Bigger than a tennis court. They'll enlarge them each year, building on new chambers and passages, fresh entrances too. You can tell how far the set stretches, because the ground sounds hollow and rattling under your feet. There'll be as many as ten separate entrances to a set. Anyway, Fred went round out of sight, and I waited. Time went on and on, and there wasn't a sound from Fred. I dursn't move, because I reckoned he must be on to something extra special. It was well after midnight, when there was a sudden hullabaloo and Fred appeared a bit red-faced asking what time it was. When he heard it was nearly one, 'Do you know', he said, 'I've been fast asleep'. It was only the badgers saw anything strange that night.

"To start with we'd leave the badgers bits of apple, cake or honey. The Latin name for badgers, *Meles meles* means honey I believe. Oh, they like sweet things all right. But it was always hard to tell exactly how much of the food the badgers had taken, or how much other animals. One night we ran out of food, and Fred happened to have a packet of them Maltesers for ourselves. We tried one or two of them on the badgers. They rushed around after them from the start. They couldn't resist them. They fought over them. After that we were friends for life. I remember some long-tailed field-mice coming after the Maltesers. The badgers soon chased them off, or got the mice too. After that we tried Smarties. Now we use unsalted peanuts. We are not quite sure what the sweets do to their teeth. We once gave one a toffee. It stuck to the roof of his mouth and we saw him struggling on his back trying to get rid of it with his paws, like a dog would do. Right drove him mad. I was feeding the badgers once and broke off a bit of chocolate that I was munching myself. The old badger wouldn't take the chocolate from me but made off with the rest of the bar still in its wrapping. There's a picture of it with the name showing in the wrapper – I reckon the firm could use it as an advertisement. You have to be careful though, metal and plastic wrappings can be very dangerous to animals, quite apart from any harm the sweets themselves might do. There's many an animal died because someone left a plastic bag out in the countryside that ended up in its stomach and blocked its innards. It's not just to be tidy that you should never leave picnic rubbish behind.

"The Smarties led us on to another experiment. There always seemed to have been doubt among naturalists as to whether badgers climbed trees. We all knew they liked to play around tree stumps, and nothing suited them better than a hollow bit of dead trunk or a fallen branch full of bugs. But no one seemed at that time to have seen, let alone photographed, a badger actually climbing a tree. So we decided to have a go with the Smarties, and one night I hid Smarties in the bark up a straight tree, just as far as I could reach, about eight foot I reckon. We didn't want to go further than that for fear the badgers might fall. We did this one or two nights, and pretty soon the badgers caught on. We could see them sniffing around the tree their noses in the air. Then one of them climbed straight up and picked off the Smarties. They went up like a cat, and came down backwards. If there was a lead off the main trunk they would turn and come down forwards. I was doing my own colour photography by then, and I got some good pictures, cine as well. I think they were the first good pictures of a badger climbing a tree, in our part of the country at any rate. There are others now. Southern TV got interested in what we were doing. A fellow who called himself Olley Kite was their big nature man, with a programme called 'Kite's Country'. He came down two or three times and we were on the air.

"Gradually the word would get around among the naturalists about our badgers and they started coming to see them. After a year or two I suppose we had about a hundred. One old lady of nearly ninety came all the way from Rye. There was one well-known man from the neighbourhood was specially keen to get photographs. He was a kind of hero of ours in them early days, Mr Walter J. C. Murray. He was a city man really, part of the rat race. Then he decided to give it all up, found an old tumble down shack Horam way, and made a nice home of it. We read his books and followed him around when he was giving talks and the like with his colour slides. One day he was doing a talk 'Creatures of the Night' I think it was, and he mentioned badgers as being very hard to photograph, them being so shy. So when he asked for questions, I wondered whether it really was so difficult, or did he need to take longer to tame them. The upshot was that if we could tame them, he'd come and photograph them. He seemed a bit doubtful and ta-tahed the whole thing.

"Anyway he finally did come, and the first time, after he'd spent quite a lot of time setting up all his equipment, it came on to rain. Badgers will go out in cold weather. I've seen their tracks in the snow. They don't hibernate, not in our part of the world. But they don't like rain and they didn't come out that night. So our friend was all the more sniffy about it. Tame badgers indeed! However we persuaded him and he did come again with his wife, saying 'Well I hope we're going to see something this time.' Well this time the badgers came out and gave a wonderful show. At the end we asked him if he'd got good pictures, and he said, 'Do you know I was so excited and flabbergasted, I quite forgot to take any pictures at all!' So he had to come the third time. Now we are good friends, and do quite a lot together. He spends time every summer with me in my hides. He still gives his nature talks and he's always on about the Rotherfield badgers.

"There's so many things I love about badgers. They are the neatest and cleanest of animals. You will find outside the entrances to their sets, not only the mountains of earth, big stones sometimes, that they have dug out to make them, but the leaves and bracken and grass that they use to line their homes and make them comfortable. They have regular spring-cleaning times, when they clear out everything, and then go out on expeditions to collect new carpeting which they roll up in balls and then drag down the entrance tunnels after them, moving backwards, and pulling the stuff in after them with their front paws. We would roll up lumps of grass and stuff and leave it for them at the entrance to their set. They would never touch it the first night. But the night after they would take it. Sometimes they have to dig the entrance tunnels right through the big mounds of earth that they have piled up over the years. They do not foul their chambers as foxes or rabbits might do. They train their young 'uns from quite an early age to use the latrines which they have dug carefully in various convenient places outside the set entrances. I've known foxes share lodgings underground with a family of badgers. But it does not seem to last long. The foxes make too much mess, and usually the old badger moves out.

"The parents do not feed their young for long or bring food home like foxes do. It is soon a case of everyone for himself. I like to see a badger ambling off on his own, or with his missus trailing along behind him, in search of food or company. He'll make a bit of a noise as he trots along with an ungainly stride, stopping at regular intervals to listen for anything going on around him. Traffic on the roads, worse still on the motorways, has broken up paths which for thousands of years have been safe and familiar badger tracks. Civilisation, so called, is always adding fresh dangers and disturbances for these shy, gentle, but very determined creatures. The huntsmen may stop up all their sets one day, putting heavy stones or fences of sticks on every hole to discourage foxes going to ground. The old badger will be a prisoner in his home. But you may be pretty sure that within a few hours, those powerful snouts and necks will be at work, and bit by bit the man-made blocks will be broken up or nuzzled away, and the badgers will be out again.

"Badgers don't give up easy. They say that they were here foraging in our forests, making their complicated underground homes, long before Britain was an island, or man knew how to make houses, or live anywhere but caves. Some people think they walked over originally from Scandinavia. One of the names for a badger is 'brock' and I believe that comes from Scandinavia. Whatever happens to man on this island of ours, I think the badgers will be somewhere around. You can bet the Rotherfield badgers will go on. I only hope there'll be some humans around to take an interest, and enjoy them as much as we do."

The Foxes

PETER does not go out of his way to talk about his adventures and discoveries about nature. He is careful not to bore other people with his knowledge and enthusiasms and needs to be sure that you really want to know. He shows a necessary caution about revealing exactly where he has seen some particular flower or bird or animal, for he knows all too well the ways of the thoughtless, ruthless bird's-nester, the wild flower picker, the hunter, the collector, and the merely casual wanderer who may interfere with a hide, trample down a quiet reserve, and destroy in a few careless moments, the patient preparations of weeks.

At the same time, if your interest is genuine, he is generous with his time. His slide shows and talks on nature are known all over our neighbourhood, and many is the time one of his shows has delighted a horticultural society, or a Women's Institute, or helped to raise money for some good cause. He will show what he has seen, but be suitably vague about just where or how he has seen it.

Like all good scholars, he is equally eager to learn something new. There is a natural fraternity between nature lovers. Information is passed on and experiences exchanged. So it happens that many a good story or strange occurrence goes the rounds. One evening Peter took a local lady who kept goats to see his badgers:

"After it was over she thanked me, and said 'Now you must come down and see my foxes.' Then she told me how, when she was milking her goats of an evening, she saw a fox sitting quietly on the steps by the goat shed waiting for her. Next day she milked her goat into a bowl on top of some bread and put it outside the goat shed. Pretty soon the fox came and took it. Now, she explained, she fed foxes regular. Well, to me, the whole thing struck me as a little bit peculiar like. A woman feeding foxes! It wasn't possible; a bit eccentric! So I took it with a pinch of salt and forgot about it.

79

"But a year later a friend said to me 'Have you been down yet to see the goat lady with her foxes?' 'I don't think I'm interested,' I said. 'Oh, but you must. I've been and it's a wonderful sight. It's as good as your badgers.' Still I couldn't believe it. A fox is such a sly, shy, clever animal; and this happening while it's still light! Impossible! But I asked the lady if I could change my mind. 'Come down,' she said, 'a couple of hours before it gets dark. I'll put you in the goat house, along with the goats, so your smell gets lost in the goat smell, and you won't scare the foxes.' So I set up my tripod and camera in the shed, and there I waited with the goats. There was no doubt whose smell was strongest! It was cramped in there too, and one of the goats kept climbing up on my shoulder looking for a nibble – they'll eat anything, you know. There was a bit of fresh air came in through a broken pane in the window, and that also gave me a good view of the green grass outside.

"Just as it was beginning to get dusk, in comes the goat lady with a bowl in her hand and some bread in it. She milks one of the goats over the bowl. Then she takes the bowl and sets it down on the grass outside where I could see it easily. 'Come on foxy' she cries with a loud voice, 'come on, foxy, no one's going to hurt you.' And, if you can believe it, two young foxes come straight out of the woods and ate the bread and milk.

"I was proper flabbergasted. 'Oh, but I wish you'd come along last year' said the lady. 'Last year these two foxes here were small cubs. They came regularly to feed with their mother. At that same time my cat had kittens. Do you know the cubs would feed out of one side of the bowl, and the kittens on the other. And in the background the vixen would watch one side, and my cat the other. If the cat got too near the bowl, the vixen would growl. And if the vixen got too near, my cat would spit. But after the cubs and kittens had finished eating, they'd play and roll around together, and the fox and the cat would share the rest of the meal. It's last year's cubs that you've seen tonight. They won't let the vixen in this year, until they've finished. When they're done, I have to call her in to get a turn.'

"I got some very good photographs, but if I ever showed pictures like

A nightjar (*Caprimulgus europaeus*) with its young. These birds use a 'scrape' rather than a nest and rely on camouflage for their protection.

Left: The little owl (*Athene noctua*) is only 22 millimetres – 9 inches – long. It can be seen in the daytime if you are lucky.
Below: A woodcock (*Scolopax rusticola*) on its nest. Its plumage is an effective camouflage.

Opposite bottom left: A caterpillar of the elephant hawk moth (*Deilephila elpenor*) photographed soon after hatching. As it gets older it turns brown.

Opposite bottom right: The buff-tip moth (*Phalera bucephala*) also popularly known, from its appearance, as the 'cigarette-end moth'.

Left: An elephant hawk moth about one hour after hatching. Its wings are not yet dry, soon the network of airspaces in them will be pumped full of air and the moth will be able to take flight.

Above: A death's-head hawk moth (*Acherontia atropos*) which gets its name from the large ochreous spot on the thorax which is shaped like a human skull.

The Rotherfield badgers

Left: The fact that badgers (*Meles meles*) can climb trees was something of a discovery when Peter first took photographs of them.

Above: The closest badger ignored the chocolate that Peter held out in his hand and made off instead with his reserve supply, the wrapper still round the bar.

The foxes

Right: Fox cubs (*Vulpes vulpes*) waiting for their mother to come home. Fox cubs are four to six weeks old before they leave the earth in which they are born.

Bottom right: Fox cubs at play. The young cubs stay in the vicinity of their den.

Far right: The vixen returns and feeding time has come at last – all the cubs rush to her to suck.

Left: A yearling fox (*Vulpes vulpes*), one of the visitors to the goat lady.
Above: A dragonfly (*Alshna cyanea*) sunning itself on a gorse bush.
Dragonflies are more likely to be found near ponds, canals and other
still waters. The swift beat of their stiff wings makes a rustling sound as
they fly.

The bog

Far left: A sundew (*Drosera rotundifolia*) growing in sphagnum moss in the bog. Its leaves are covered with sticky glands that can trap insects which they then curl around and digest.

Top left: A meadow or solitary thistle (*Cirsium dissectum*), one of the thistles that is without prickles.

Bottom left: The nest of a snipe (*Gallinago gallinago*) with four eggs. The eggs are laid in spring or summer. The chicks hatch in three weeks and three weeks later begin to make the swift sudden flights which make them so difficult to shoot.

Above: A common spotted orchid (*Dactylorhiza fuchsii*) together with a crab spider (*Misumena vatia*).

Above right: The flower of the bog asphodel (*Narthecium ossifragum*). The deep orange seed heads of this plant make attractive decorations.

Right: The bog pimpernel (*Anagallis tenella*) is rare in our parts but forms a creeping groundcover in the bog.

The old railway

Far left: The defunct railway is carpeted with buttercups (*Ranunculus sp*), ox-eye daisies (*Leucanthemum vulgare*) and birdsfoo trefoil (*Lotus corniculatus*).

Left: Wild strawberries (*Fragaria vesca*) can be plentiful alon the old railway track

Left below: Toadflax (*Linaria vulgaris*) is common weed on roadsides and railway banks.

Top right: Berries of the guelder rose (*Viburnum opulus*), which grows over six feet tall in hedges and at wood edges.

Bottom right: A robin's powder puff or pin cushion, a gall caused by an insect laying its eggs on wild rose stems.

Top far right: An early purple orchid (*Orchis mascula*), first of our orchids to appear in spring.

Bottom far right: Honeysuckle (*Lonicera periclymenum*), or woodbine, grows to enormous lengths twining clockwise around any plant or young tree.

Top left: A male common blue butterfly (*Polyommatus icarus*) the female is brown.

Bottom left: A brimstone butterfly (*Goneptoryx rhamni*). The male is bright sulphur-yellow, the female paler with a greenish tinge.

Above: A small pearl-bordered fritillary (*Boloria selene*) which favours marshy ground and flies fast.

Right: The long-tailed tit (*Aegithalos caudatus*) is a magnificent nest-builder, lining it with perhaps a thousand tiny feathers.

Far right top: A chiffchaff (*Phylloscopus collybita*), first of our spring migrants from Africa.

Far right bottom: A dunnock or hedge sparrow (*Prunella modularis*) feeding its young.

that people might think the foxes were from a zoo or something. I've never heard of anything like it all the same.

"The first time I photographed a fox I was in a field with bullocks. As usual the bullocks were all nuzzling around. So as I got closer to the fox, I was in among the bullocks, so the fox didn't bother about me. I got quite close, click, and there was another first. Animals don't disturb other animals, unless they are hunting food. Cars, planes, tractors are all accepted. It's a funny thing but railway lines and even motorways often act as nature reserves, just because man doesn't often go there on foot and doesn't interfere, except of course by running animals over. It's only the two legged animal that's the enemy, man. Sad really. We must take a walk along the old disused Rotherfield railway line some time, and I'll show you what I mean.

"I'm very proud of one of my fox pictures. It's of a vixen feeding a whole litter of cubs. I'd waited years to get that picture. Like all those things, it's a matter of luck and planning. First of all, of course, you have to find where the foxes are. That's easy. You've only got to go where you find white feathers picked out of the tail of birds, or bits of rabbit or rabbit's fur or chicken bone and the like. Then you know from the time of year (I reckon this was April or May) that the young'uns are probably down there, while the dog fox and vixen are likely to be out hunting food. If you're lucky the mother might come back to feed the cubs.

"You have to prepare things a bit, flatten the grass and bracken down around the fox hole, so you'll get a better view, if they come. This I'd done some weeks earlier when the bracken began to grow. Then I climbed a tree. If you were to be on the ground the vixen would be able to smell you. If she did, she'd make a wide circle round the earth, creating and hollering. A vixen will make a weird noise if her cubs are threatened – it's like her mating call but more sharp and emphatic. I've even seen one right up on her hind legs screaming. You'd never see the littl'uns then. But if you're up a tree, the smell goes upwards, and the vixen doesn't know you're there.

"You might have to wait up there for quite a time so you need to make yourself comfortable. No use jumping or wriggling about just

A dunnock or hedge sparrow (*Prunella modularis*) feeding a cuckoo in its nest. This bird is often the victim of the cuckoo. Sometimes it will fly on to the cuckoo's back in its attempts to feed it.

when the fun's beginning. But this was my lucky day. It was about eleven o'clock in the morning. In a quarter of an hour or so the cubs came out, and started to play. I was snapping away. But about three quarters of an hour later, up came the vixen. And if you can believe it, there were ten cubs fighting around her to get her milk. And I got the pictures. I don't know if they could have all been one litter. I never saw signs of another vixen. I've never seen anything like it before or since, and I've known foxes almost all my life.

"I must have been nine or ten years old when my brother said to me, 'Why don't you follow the hounds on foot? You can go places you wouldn't be allowed otherwise, and you can notice the birds and animals as you go. You can see where the rabbits are too, and that can come in useful when we go out poaching.' So I started following the hounds. Every Saturday I'd be home late after six o'clock and get a thrashing from my Dad. Every Saturday I'd be out again. I was told not to go but I still went. And I can truly say I've followed the Eridge Hunt regularly, once, often twice a week for fifty-five years ever since. It's not the hunting I care about really, it's all the things along the way. I've hardly ever been at a kill in my life. Not that there are scarcely any with the Eridge. The country's too broken up to chase a fox as far as all that! And if he gets away, you've lost him for good. They seldom catch a sly old Eridge fox in full chase. If they ever do, it's probably a very old one. No, I don't care so much for the meets either. I get to know where they're going, and I pick them up on foot and spend a good day out in the open, listening to the hounds and watching them working. I often say that when I'm following the music of the hounds, it's like an engine on the back of my bike, or if I'm running, I feel ten years younger.

"When I was young, I would have to walk to wherever the meet was. It might be ten miles away or more. Then later on I put together my first bike. I got two old wheels off a rubbish heap. No tyres, mind, and no pedals. But I gradually found bits and pieces. I still go by bike to the Hunt, wherever it's meeting. I leave the bike somewhere convenient and then follow on foot. My Wednesdays and Saturdays are booked for following. I don't have to work those days now.

"There's always something new to look out for. Just the other day

four deer suddenly came out of nowhere. They are escapees from Eridge Park. You used to see a lot of them before they cut down so many of the big trees. Then when the firs were planted, they would be around eating the tips off the young trees. Now the firs have grown, it's harder to see them.

"Oh, the hunt's always interesting. I never get tired of it. I must have run and walked thousands and thousands of miles with the hunt. A lot of first class naturalists go along, just for what they can see by the way. This time of year, with the spring coming on, I'm looking out for all my 'firsts.' The first primrose, the first daffodil, coltsfoot, kingcups and the rest. Then there's the first brimstone butterfly – we saw that in your garden last week – and the first tortoiseshell too, and the first blackbird nesting. The first migrant birds to arrive are the chiffchaffs, then the willow warblers. Swallows come later. I note them all down in a book and see how the record compares with last year and the years before that.

"The Hunt made me an honorary member, you know. I suppose I've made myself useful, opening gates, shutting them, and so on. Yes, I've got the letter somewhere. 'For conscientious following of the hounds.' That's what it says, or something of the kind. The Master of the Hunt of that time gave me a button. He's supposed to cut one off his own coat, really. But he fished one out of his pocket. 'Do you mind having this,' he said. 'It'll save my wife having to sew on another.'

"I've seen the Queen and the Queen Mother at the Eridge Hunt and I've seen Prince Charles and Princess Anne. They were in a land-rover. He was having a terrible job trying to back it in the mud, and his sister was laughing at him, and teasing him good and proper. No, I'd never take a picture of them, nor interfere in any way. I'm out for wild life, not high life. Besides, out in these parts, they're just country folk, like we are. Let 'em get on with it. And we do the same. We're all ordinary people then.

"To tell you the truth, I've no time for a fox. It is the cruellest of animals. It will kill twenty chickens and only take one. The rest it kills for fun, same as a cat will play with a mouse or bird. But they are clever all right. When a hunt is on, I've seen a fox sit quietly waiting right in the middle of a field, and then go deliberately towards the hounds so as to confuse the scent. It will climb up in the rhododendrons, where the hounds can't smell, take to water or mix with sheep to hide its traces. I've never seen a worried-looking fox.

"One thing you can say for them is that they are very good parents. For most of the year they lead solitary lives, but in mid-winter, when the mating season comes along, the dog fox seeks out his mate. You can hear his sharp bark *'yap, yap, yap* – three times. Sometimes I've heard him bark only twice, *'yap, yap,'* like a knock on the door. Then the vixen answers with that wild, eerie howling. Several dog foxes will fight over one vixen. Once they're mated, they make an earth. They don't dig fresh like a badger will. Nothing so neat and tidy. They'll usually pick on some hole that's already there, a big rabbit hole for instance. Then they'll enlarge it and settle in. Or they may take over a disused badger set, or even a set with badgers in it, and make themselves at home at the opposite end to the badgers. The cubs are born in early spring. Then the parents go out hunting for food. The dog fox will bring food to the vixen, who then takes it to the cubs. The dog fox isn't allowed too near the earth at feeding time when the cubs are very young. But I've seen a dog fox with a big chicken in its mouth come within sight of the vixen. The fox was pretty well dead tired; almost done in. He'd keep putting the chicken down, stagger a bit, then pick it up and struggle on a few steps at a time. The smaller creatures he'll sling over his shoulder. It's not long before the cubs learn to do the same, and you can see them with a tiny rabbit slung over their backs as they take it down the hole.

"It seems there comes a time when the old dog fox gets tired of being the family provider. Did you see that TV programme showing a family of foxes living in a cellar under a house? You saw the male bringing in food for his mate and for the cubs. And then one day they'd got to start fending for themselves. He came in, put the food down as usual, and then he took a good hard look at his wife, turned around and ate the food himself. Then he ran out and the Missus followed him. She'd have to do her own foraging from then on.

"You know a vixen will bury food before she has her cubs so that she doesn't have to leave them to go out hunting.

"Back in the days before I was doing any photographing, a friend asked me if I knew of any place where he could get pictures of young foxes. Well I knew a place by a stream, with banks on either side. Foxes often make their earth close to a stream. We were watching up on higher ground some way away from the fox holes, looking down with field-glasses, when a vixen came out through a hedge and was running down towards the earth. It didn't see us, but suddenly halfway down the field, it started to scream and give its warning note. I thought she had smelt us, but it wasn't us. She went straight to one of the fox holes, and there, sticking out of the entrance was the hindquarters of an Airedale dog scratching away. That vixen grabbed hold of the dog and was nipping it good and proper. Pretty soon a fight started, and the Airedale ran away. But the vixen chased it in figures of eight all up and down a couple of fields. Every time it caught up with the dog it would give another nip, and the dog would yap, yap. I met the owner of the dog sometime later, told him what I'd seen and said 'How is your cowardly dog?' 'Oh well,' said the owner, 'He's a jolly good house dog.'

"It's the mother, not the father fox, who'll risk her life for her young. After all, the dog fox might well have a couple of wives and families or even three, mightn't he? Mother love is a powerful instinct in animals. I've seen a rabbit even tackle a stoat, that was threatening her young'uns.

"I don't think a fox would ever attack a person, not really. But I do remember one night with Fred, back in our fox-watching days. Fred was photographing then, and we were right close to the place where the badgers are now. I don't think the badgers were there then. Anyway we were hiding down in a big hole with only our heads visible. A fox and vixen saw us, just our heads. They must have thought we were some kind of smallish animal. They could only see our heads. Suddenly, they started to growl and began making straight for us. I tell you it was something to see that long pointed nose, those tall ears, glinting eyes and sharp pointed teeth coming right at you. 'Stand up' I shouted to Fred, and we didn't waste time scrambling to our feet. As soon as they saw what we were, they made off fast. For a moment or two it was the hunt the other way round. Only fair, when you come to think of it!"

The Bog

IT WAS the end of October and there had been big winds and storms in the night. Peter turned up and said "Why don't we go and have a look at the bog?"

"Why the bog?" I said, looking at the rain-filled clouds scudding by. The bog always struck me as rather a derelict spot. I had memories of going there with my mother during the First World War, while she and other ladies of the village gathered sphagnum moss, which was used to make soft, hygienic dressings for the wounded.

"The garden's bog enough today," I thought, but a trip out with Peter is seldom wasted and we set out, Peter sharing his knowledge as we walked:

"The bog's a wonderful spot for some of the rare finds. I reckon to go there at least every month. There's a dragonfly we discovered down on the bog that all the experts thought was extinct in Sussex. They were proper excited when we showed it to them. Tell you the truth, I think there are people who would like to buy the bog, and fence it in. Trouble is, when you do that you can destroy the very things you are aiming to protect. With a fence around the bog the cattle would no longer be able to get in to trample down the willow and suchlike. In a few years the whole place would be overgrown, and all the small, rare flowers would be smothered. No, me and my mates hope they'll leave the bog as it is. After all, it's probably been the way it is for hundreds, even thousands of years. It's too soft and wet to plough. The soil is too acid and peaty to be good for planting. Of course there won't be much to see this time of year, but you may as well get the feel of the place."

We made our way down towards the district of Jarvis Brook, where the stream that gives it its name seeps down through the bog to join with other streams and eventually flow into the Medway and the sea. Turning off this road by an old water-works, we followed a track across the "water-splash", an old ford of the Jarvis Brook, that is sometimes swollen deep by rain. From there we took to the open fields, watched suspiciously both by herds of Sussex short-horns and by the local farmer. He welcomes nature lovers, but quite recently he had some of his cattle stolen by rustlers driving up with a truck at night.

Peter is right about the bog. It has an air of its own, primeval, unchanging. The very earliest evidence of life has been discovered here. During some tunnelling excavations, made by the Crowborough Water Company in 1906, two enormous bird footprints were found some ninety feet below the present level of the ground. The marks left by these two clawed feet are three times the size of an ostrich foot and they cover a span of two yards in their stride. Geologists claim that a great river flowed through the Jarvis Brook valley in those days, when England was part of the continent and the mammoth and the woolly rhinoceros roamed the land.

Council housing estates have crept up rather close to the bog on one side and the railway line runs along by the stream at the other, but the unyielding bog, a narrow strip of scrub and mud, bounded on the north by the forest and on the south by farm and development land, remains intact, some 100 yards wide and 300 yards long.

By this time the rain was coming down hard again, so we took shelter under a tree, while Peter helped me imagine the bog on warmer, sunnier days. What seemed like wasteland to most people was for him a natural treasure house.

"Mind you, you have to be careful when you're studying the bog. I've never known it to dry up, not even in the record dry summer of 1976. When a naturalist friend of ours came over that year to take some pictures, we warned him to watch himself. But everything looked so parched and dry, that he pooh-poohed us, took off his shoes and walked straight in. He hadn't gone more than a few steps than he was in over his knees. He didn't half pong when we finally got him out.

"You see that long black ridge there, over to the right. Not a thing has grown on that ground, not even a blade of grass. That's part of the old shooting range that was set up during the First World War for the

Dad's Army of those days to get shooting practice in order to defend their country. I guess there's too much lead in there for anything to grow.

"If we walk down the slope we might put up a snipe. They nest in the grass close to water, near the mud, where they can probe with those long bills of theirs and find worms and beetles and such-like. You'll specially see snipe in the winter, and some of them have come in from the north of Europe. They'll probably lie low, and not get up unless you're almost on top of them. You know that zig-zag flight of the snipe. You reckon yourself to be a pretty good shot if you can hit one. It will mark out its territory with a series of sudden dives. As it comes down it will make a strange noise with its tail feathers, it's like the bleating of a young goat. You can recognise a snipe by its long beak which it thrusts deep into the mud. The tip of its bill is especially sensitive to help it find its food.

"Another, much smaller, bird that nests and feeds in this part is the reed bunting. They are real performers. They have an elaborate courting ritual, first in the air and then suddenly down on the ground, with the male parading around the female like a soldier in full uniform. I've seen a reed bunting put on an act when anyone threatens their nest. They'll limp along as though they were lame, to act as a decoy, and then suddenly take flight again before they can be caught. The male has a black head with a white collar and is sometimes known as the parson; white whiskers is another name.

"You find some unusual flowers growing in the bog. This year we had a beautiful purple patch of meadow thistle, or, as we call it, solitary thistle. There's just one thistle on a stalk, and no prickles. It only lasts about a week. It seems to be rare in our part of the world. The marsh violet, only an inch or two tall and a nice covering on marshy ground, is another one that is commoner in the north than it is around here. We've found it here, but it has none of that lovely scent. One of the rarest flowers for us is the bog pimpernel. This is another nice creeper and ground coverer. It also belongs to the north and to Wales and Ireland, and we don't know how it got to us. Maybe it comes on the hooves of cattle, or snipe could have brought it. Snipe could hide and carry a lot on those long bills of their's, or on their feet.

"Another interesting flower in the bog is the sundew. The long spindly stalks and small white flowers are nothing much. It's the leaves that make it so special because they're covered with sticky red hairs, which are for trapping insects. If a fly lands on them the leaves curl inwards, trapping it, and the sticky hairs exude digestive juices which break down the victim's body. Then the plant can absorb it as food. This is how the sundew gets the nitrogen salts it needs, and supplements its food so that it can grow in the bog's acid soil. The enemies of insects are everywhere. I happened to get a picture of a spotted orchid with a crab spider on it. 'Two for the price of one' I call it.

"Do you remember me showing you that spider's nest lined with the finest web, and a web spread out in front of it like a welcome mat? I barely touched that web with a blade of grass and like lightning a big black spider shot out to grab its prey. It must have been hungry that day. All the different kinds of spider have a whole armoury of weapons for catching their victims. There are the sticky spiders' webs we all know, with threads so fine that, thickness for thickness, they are harder to break than iron. Other spiders catch their prey by jumping on them, some spit out gummy threads. Others build tube-like webs in the ground, and can stab their victims and drag them down under to eat. I've seen that. There's even a spider that lives and hunts under water. Though that I've never seen.

"Of course, our big find in the bog has been our own special dragonfly. The powder blue darter is its proper name. That is a real beauty, with a wonderful blue sparkle in the sunlight. Its special feature is the way its upper wings point forward instead of stretching out horizontal. There are modern 'planes that follow this pattern with wings pointed forward. As soon as we spotted this one we knew it was a rarity, so we reported it to the Sussex Trust. You'd probably be surprised to know that there's an organised Sussex Dragonfly Survey. They've recorded 32 different species of dragonfly in Sussex. Our powder blue darter is mentioned as only to be found in a small bog near Crowborough. They are afraid of its total extinction, so we are asked to keep a special eye on it. Dragonflies are supposed to be some of the oldest insects in the world. There are fossilised remains millions of years old.

"Have you ever seen one coming out of its nymph? I've managed to get a nice picture of that too. The nymphs they hatch from live in mud at the bottom of ponds or slow moving streams. The nymphs look so ugly that it is hard to believe that they will become something so beautiful. They can lie down there for a year or even five years at a time, feeding on tadpoles and the like. When the time comes at last to hatch, the nymph will slowly climb up the stem of a plant out of water. Then it will shed its skin and dry out its wings. After an hour or so, it will fly away as a fully fledged grown-up. Probably a month later its life will be over. What a long time to prepare for such a short life! But for those few weeks what speed, what beauty! They say that dragonflies can travel anything up to sixty miles an hour, though that's probably a bit of an exaggeration.

"This rain is getting you thoroughly soaked! We'll come back again in the summer. I bet there's not so many in Rotherfield even know that the bog exists. And yet for me it's one of the strangest and most interesting spots within my three mile area."

The Old Railway Line

IT WAS just after Wimbledon, 1978, rather a wet one too. No sooner was the tournament over than the sulky skies cleared for a while, and for the first time in weeks there was summer sun to warm your back. Peter and I decided to take a walk along the old railway line between Rotherfield and Mayfield. For me there is something haunted about such a place, the shining rails long since removed, a tunnel, whose mouth once belched smoke and roared like thunder, now hollow and silent, the deep cutting overgrown with towering bushes, blackberries and wild roses.

There is a giant disused railway bridge, three spans wide and as high as a vaulted cathedral. It was a monumental piece of engineering built just for the sake of carts and cattle belonging to a farm that had been cut in two by the railway. It now towers mute and desolate, a prey to vandals who tear out the bricks one by one and hurl them into the tangled undergrowth, or perhaps take them away for purposes of their own. The whole place is full of ghosts, relics of an empty shrine once dedicated to the great god steam, a god now dethroned but still remembered with excitement and some awe. I heard of someone long ago walking at night, when a late train, shooting out sparks, puffed its way up the steep gradient to Rotherfield Station. The man came running into the village screaming. "I've seen the devil let loose in Hornshurst woods."

They called this "The Cuckoo Line" on account of the annual Cuckoo Fair at Heathfield, one of the chief stations. The saying is that on April 15th "the old woman of Heathfield lets the cuckoo out of her cage."

A hundred years ago the quiet, secluded spot where we were standing now must have been alive with the clang of sledge-hammers driving in spars, the shouts of the navvies as they laid the shining metal, harsh foreign tongues, straining backs and heavy work well done. The new Tunbridge Wells and Eastbourne Railway Company were hard at it. The steep one track line snaked its way up and over, down and round and through the heavily wooded Wealden hills. Then came the great opening day. September 1st 1880. Trim Victorian stations, railway yards and cottages had been given a final lick of paint. The narrow signal boxes were at the ready with neat rows of heavy levers to work the signals and shift the points. Mysterious little bells heralded the arrival of the very first train to go "down the cuckoo" as railwaymen called it. As the train on our line entered the single track at Redgate Mill, we children would watch fascinated as the signalman came down from his box and handed a heavy wooden staff, ringed with brass, to the train driver, who would take it without quite stopping the train. This was his passport through the Cuckoo Line. No two trains could run at the same time.

The building of the railways in the nineteenth century reshaped our countryside. They snatched away much of nature, with their long fingers bringing the suburbs far out into the open country, with their viaducts and bridges, their huge sheds, and railway stations, and all the vast building that went with them. However the railways which took away so much have given back also. Railway lines can be nature reserves, With frequent high embankments sheltering them from wind and storm, protected from human interference, often mowed only by scythe, they form a kind of sanctuary. Now, where branch lines like ours have been closed down, their quiet cuttings and undisturbed ways are bursting with plants and wildlife.

"It's a good place for flowers, birds and butterflies," said Peter. "I reckon to come along here every three or four weeks or so. In the spring it's all yellow with primroses, cowslips and Lent lilies. Bit by bit it changes to the pinks and whites of summer, the wild roses and the willowherb. Later in autumn it's bright red with the hips and the haws and the bryony berries. So you come to winter with frost and snow, and the white hairy-covered seeds of old man's beard. Remember how we climbed down here in the mud to pick old man's beard for your daughter's wedding. It makes a good decoration for a December wedding, along with Christmas holly.

"We could get a punnet of wild strawberries here easy. I'd trespass down along here as a boy sometimes, and see what I could pick up. In those days they'd keep the banks along the railway neat and tidy. I've seen them cutting and haying the grass and piling it into goods' trucks to take down to Eastbourne and Brighton to feed the horses which pulled the delivery vans.

"Look at those wild roses now. They are just about at their best. Must be thousands of them. They seem mostly white one side of the cutting and pink the other. People always used to wear a pink rose like that in their buttonhole on Alexandra Day. Do you see that red mossy ball, covered in yellowish fluff, growing on a rose bush? That's what we call a robin's powder-puff. Robin's pin-cushion, I believe, is another name. It's caused by a type of gall wasp which lays its eggs in the bud or in the leaf tissue which, instead of developing normally, grows to form the gall. They form the food for the developing larvae and don't cause much harm to the plant. You sometimes get them on garden roses but much more often on wild ones. In the middle ages they used to be broken into powder and used as a treatment for bladder stones and other diseases.

"I expect you know that plant with the double round leaves, like two of the old pennies side by side. We call it money-wort. It's probably an 'escape' from some garden, or even from a passing train. You get plants along here that usually grow on chalk, like that blue chicory. You can mix its roots with coffee. They probably come from the Downs at the other end of the line. They could blow off open goods trucks, or come with the flints which they used to line the tracks. Those purple flowers there are cranesbill, a wild form of geranium. They used to say that this plant dried in the oven and mixed with nine red slugs would cure rupture in old people. Of course plants and herbs were everybody's medicine in the old days. And they are still used today. Morphine is manufactured from poppies, and the heart medicine, digitalis, comes from foxgloves. Those yellow flowers there are trefoil. There are many sorts. That one there is birdsfoot trefoil. We call it 'bread and cheese'. Don't know why!

"You'll know that tall purple plant with green leaves from arrangements of winter flowers. It's a teasel. It's the plant they used to use for raising the nap on newly woven cloth. Teasling, they call it. Another plant around here that has connections with the clothing industry is the burdock. Its burrs stick together similarly to the velcro fastener in modern coats. It's supposed to have given the inventor the idea.

"Yes, that tall weed there is poison alright. It's a form of hemlock, though I doubt if it's the same they used to give people in the old days. You'll find that horsetail with the single spikes growing in water and damp places. They had to drain the line here. There's a broken bit left of the old piping they used. These are fine big daisies aren't they? Horse daisies we call them. Ox-eye is another name. There's a bit of wild carrot, and that hog-weed there is related to parsley. There's all kind of different vetch. I reckon we could spend a week here and never get to the end of it.

"There was an accident on the line on September 1st 1897. Too great a speed on the sharp curves and grades near Mayfield brought about a derailment, with the Bonchurch engine and a single coach sprawled on its side. I can remember the notice as you approached Mayfield. 'Speed not to exceed 20 miles an hour.' There was quite a lot of goods' traffic in the old days, with coal and building materials, and of course the early milk train. Farmers drove their carts to the various stations with their big milk churns. I still seem to hear the rumble of the heavy churns being rolled along the platforms and the clang as they were heaved into the van. Then there is the quick slam of the door, the guard's whistle, and the engine's reply, a shrill toot, with a quick succession of puffs, as the wheels grip on the rails.

"I was down by the railway one dark night when the trains were still running. You remember that hiss of escaping steam you used to get as it got to the crest of the hill toward Rotherfield Station. It was that peculiar hiss that must have disturbed a fox, because it ran out and went straight between my legs. I closed my legs and held it there for quite a moment or two. I don't know which of us was the most shocked and surprised, me or the fox.

"This is a good stretch for butterflies. Pretty soon it will be full of red admirals and tortoiseshells, peacocks and painted ladies. There are far fewer butterflies on the whole than there used to be. Take the white admiral. At one time this beautiful butterfly was very common in Sussex, so much so that it was chosen as the emblem of the Sussex Trust. Later it disappeared entirely in our district. Now some are back again just on one patch not too far from here. But I'm not telling where – we don't want to lose them again. The caterpillar of the white admiral seals itself up in a leaf with silk during the winter and is ready to pupate and come out as a butterfly in June or July. Now the red admiral is quite different. It's a migrant. It flies in all the way from the Mediterranean countries. How it finds its way and survives wind and storm nobody really knows. The scientists do all kinds of experiments with migrating birds and butterflies to try and discover how they navigate, whether it's by the sun or the stars, or whether it's by some inner mechanism all their own. People invent special devices to block up the sight or hearing

Autumn near Rotherfield. In Nap Wood on Saxonbury Hill.

In the woods

Left: The male cones or flowers of a pine (*Pinus sylvestris*).
Top: The male flowers of the oak (*Quercus robur*).
Above: The male flowers of the yew (*Taxus baccata*) appear in February.
Female trees have green flowers growing along the branches.

Right: A wasps' nest.
Far right: The saw wort (*Serratula tinctoria*).
Below: Heather, or ling (*Erica tetralix*), grows well on the poorer, more acid soil of the higher ground around Rotherfield. A solitary gentian is growing amongst it.
Below right: The slowworm or blindworm (*Anguis fragilis*) is neither blind nor a worm. It is a legless lizard. If caught by the tail it can leave part of it behind and grow a new one.

Left: The female cone or flower of the larch (*Larix decidua*).
Below left: Wood spurge (*Euphorbia amygdaloides*).
Below: Cuckoo pint (*Arum maculatum*), also known as lords and ladies and wild arum.
Right: The cuckoo pint in late summer with its poisonous fruit.
Bottom right: The wood anemone (*Anemone nemorosa*) which flowers early.
Far right: An adder (*Vipera berus*), the only poisonous snake in Britain.

Far left: A male kestrel (*Falco tinnunculus*) on its nest forty-feet up in a Scots pine. The male has a blue-grey head and tail but the female has the same mottled brown as the wings and back. This is the most common bird of prey in Britain and Europe. Their hovering flight, wings flickering and tail spread, helps to identify them as they hang in the air looking for prey. Kestrels often lay their eggs directly on the ledge of a cliff or tall building, or take over an old crow's nest instead of building their own.

Left: The chicks in the kestrel nest at three weeks old.

Above: The kestrel chicks at six weeks old.

A green woodpecker (*Picus viridis*) one of our noisiest birds. As well as the hammer, hammer of its powerful beak, digging its nest in tree trunks or telegraph poles, this bird has a loud, laughing call that gives it its popular name of the yaffle. There is a country tradition that its cry is '*wet, wet, wet*' when there is going to be rain. It is also known as the galleybird, for it leans back like the figurehead on a ship.

A starling (*Sturnus vulgaris*) is a bird that can adapt easily and make itself at home anywhere. This bird has made its nest in the hole dug out by the woodpecker in the preceding picture, moving in the following year, for woodpeckers make a new nest-hole each year. Starlings, many of them migrants from the continent, foul city buildings as they seek the warmth of towns. They also damage crops and fruit.

Left: A cock chaffinch (*Fringilla coelebs*) on its nest. These birds came in large numbers to the newly planted conifer trees of local afforestation but disappeared again when the small trees grew bigger.

Right: A bullfinch (*Pyrrhula pyrrhula*) nesting in the newly-planted conifers.

Below: The skylark (*Alauda arvensis*) is one of the great singing birds, sustaining a warbling song as it soars and hovers. Then, silent, it finally drops to earth like a stone.

Above: A jay (*Garrulus glandarius*) with chicks at its nest in an old laurel. The jay is shy and difficult to approach at close quarters but its harsh squawk at the approach of strangers or intruders has earned it the name of 'watchman of the woods'.

Right: A nuthatch (*Sitta europea*) nests in holes and will plaster up part of the entrance with mud to make it just the size it wants. This is the only British bird that habitually climbs down a tree headfirst in its search for insects in the bark. The woodpecker comes down backwards and the tree creeper climbs up as it feeds and then flies down to the foot to start again.

Far right: Peter, with his bicycle, turns homeward on an autumn evening.

Top left: The chanterelle (*Cantharellus cibarius*) is a fungus with an almost flower-like shape. It is not only a delicate apricot colour – it smells like apricot too and it is good to eat.

Bottom left: Young fruit-bodies of the fungus *Hypholoma sublateritium*.

Above: The fly agaric (*Amanita muscaria*) is a fungus usually found in association with birch trees. It looks like a sundae sprinkled with icing or nuts: but do not eat it – it is poisonous.

Above right: The panther cap (*Amanita pantherina*) has a similar shape to the fly agaric. Although its muted colours lack the warning red, beware! It is even more poisonous.

Right: A bracket fungus (*Laetiporus sulphureus*) growing on a dead yew.

Far right: The stagshorn fungus (*Calocera viscosa*) which commonly grows on the stumps of firs.

of the poor creatures or confuse them by human interference. I don't know whether they'll get much nearer the truth. I prefer to let some of these things stay a mystery. There will always be things in nature that we humans cannot explain or understand.

"Well, to get back to the red admiral, when it arrives it lays its eggs on nettles, not because it likes nettles, but because nettles are what will suit the caterpillar for food when it hatches out. Later in the summer the butterflies come out and you'll see lots of them sunning themselves along here, or on the buddleia in your garden. The painted lady is another delicate and beautiful butterfly that migrates here in the summer. The new butterflies that come out later in the summer cannot survive the cold winter and some migrate again to the south. You wonder why they make these tremendous journeys, when you'd think they would be better off in the sunnier lands they come from.

"Now tortoiseshells and peacocks are different again. They will hibernate during the winter in sheltered places, or even in the corner of an old barn. A day in winter that's unusually mild and sunny will rouse one of these creatures up – so that you might see one fluttering around on Christmas day. It is not always easy to get good photos of a peacock butterfly, because it rests with its wings closed, but it will sometimes open them up, if it senses an enemy approaching, so that those beautiful big eyes on its wings will help to scare it away.

"You'll hear some lovely bird song along the old line. Those blackberry bushes are full of linnet and bullfinch nests. And listen, that sharp, high, piercing note is a wren. It's the smallest of birds, and it's got the loudest song. This is good country for wrens. With it's tiny body and strong legs and beak a wren can move in and out of all this thick, tangled growth, with nooks and crannies full of insects and spiders where the larger birds find it harder to go. There's a blackbird giving an alarm note. We're intruders here. Seldom people about. The birds have it mostly to themselves.

"That lower, more reedy call – that's the willow tit. They like the damp down here, and the willows that have grown up so quickly since the railway went."

Sunbeams penetrating foliage and the woodland floor have always attracted Peter's photographer's eye.

"It sounds like the oboe to the wren's flute and piccolo," I said. "And look! There's an apple tree and it's full of pretty nice apples".

"Now you noticed that and I didn't" said Peter. "I bet it came from an apple core someone threw out of the carriage window long ago. You wouldn't have an apple tree growing otherwise, practically on top of the line. Perhaps you or I threw that one out when we were boys."

My mind went racing back over the years. Sunday school outings. Special reserved carriages. Sometimes even a whole train. Crowds of excited children, spades and buckets, sandwiches, sweets, apples and ginger beer ("Good pop this. Doesn't repeat"). Voluminous bathing costumes, pink rubber bathing caps, flannel bags rolled up over the knee, grey felt sunhats, sand shoes and shrimping nets. And then on the way home, sand in the half-eaten sandwiches, sodden towels and bedraggled socks and stockings, much laughter mixed with just a few tears and tummy aches.

On June 14th 1965 the line was closed. An imaginative Sussex builder has turned Rotherfield Station into a modern and desirable private residence. The old lamp-room is an up-to-date kitchen; the former waiting-room is a spacious dining room with a fifteen-foot vaulted ceiling. The space between the two platforms, which alternately witnessed my grudging good-bye waves and my wild greeting when I came home from school, has now become an elegant sunken garden with a long white swimming pool.

"They weren't bad builders in those days." We had reached the bridge with its beautifully shaped and rounded arches. Peter does not restrict his appreciation entirely to nature. "Only last night I saw a programme on television, where a lady won a raffle to blow up a bridge like that one. She pulled the switch and the top of the arch came down, but the uprights stood firm. They knew how to make 'em then. And no modern cranes or electric shovels to help them neither. The lady said she'd rather have left it alone and let creepers grow up it. Well, nature comes back in the end.

"Now, that's where we climb back up to the road again. Watch yourself, don't get caught on the brambles."

In the Woods

THE WOODS around Rotherfield have changed greatly since Peter and I were young. In the past the Rotherfield woods were part of the Marquis of Abergavenny's Estate. They consisted of stately oaks and beeches, with great pools of bluebells in spring and waves of golden bracken in autumn. The woods were free for any who wished to roam, and trips to the woods to pick flowers, picnic or collect firewood were part of the life of most Rotherfield inhabitants. This could not always have been so. In the Domesday Book only two holdings in Sussex are entered as William the Conqueror's personal estates, one at Bosham and one at Rotherfield. In the entry for the Rotherfield Hundred it is specifically stated: "There is a park."

This park was evidently reserved for the royal hunt, and was probably situated around Hornshurst Woods, where the name Park Wood is preserved. There are still place-names like Maynard's Gate, Redgate, High Gate, Blackthorngate round Rotherfield. This suggests that the area was enclosed. The King, who was a keen huntsman did not wish to be disturbed by trespassers, nor for his deer or boar to be poached or to escape into open country. Now the enclosure system has, to some extent, come again. The Abergavenny family have sold most of their estate. The woods have been bought by timber companies. The great old trees have been replaced by thickly planted conifers: Norway spruce, fir, larch and pine, and the whole area is shut in by padlocked gates. But the Marquis still takes a great personal interest in tree-planting.

However, there are still several public footpaths and rights of way which, though not easily defined, are jealously preserved. In any case, Peter Warnett is granted the honorary freedom of the woods, just as he is of the Eridge Hunt.

Fortunately parts of the old woodland remain within Peter's three-mile limit. The timber companies have deliberately left some of the old trees. There is also Nap Wood, on Saxonbury Hill, a splendid area of forest, which has been presented to the National Trust and is carefully preserved by the Sussex Trust. Peter is on the Nap Wood Committee, and he has been responsible for putting up and watching sixty-three bird boxes there.

The new woodlands are not much to Peter's liking:

"Well, of course I'd rather have the old trees than this reforestation. This part of the country is wonderful for the oak and the beech. Round here you see them at their finest. When they were building the great hall at Westminster, back in the days of the Normans, it's thought that they took the wood for the roof from Lord Courthope's estate at Wadhurst not far from here. And when that great roof needed to be repaired between the wars due to death watch beetle it was Lord Courthope's descendant, who gave oak, from the same woods, to be used again.

"There's an old country saying 'An oak takes a hundred years growing and a hundred years dying'. It's often longer than that I reckon. Oaks are a home and a larder for thousands of creatures, even long after the tree has died. You should be careful about clearing away dead trees. You may lose a lot of birds and other creatures if you do.

"Many fine beeches have been felled lately, not just because of the new planting, but because they are supposed to be a threat to traffic on the roads, after they reach a certain age. All the same it was a terrible shock when a great cathedral of beeches covering the whole road between Eridge and Tunbridge Wells was all cut down. It was like losing part of your home. It's true beech wood does tend to split after a certain age, but when you lose that fresh green of the beech in spring, and the gold of the autumn leaves, you've lost a friend. And there's nothing like the cool, dark shade of the beech in summer, and the clean, leafy carpet, where few plants grow except for the bird's nest orchid and one or two other flowers.

"At the same time you've got to admit that with the new planting

there are gains as well as losses. We're apt to lose the birds that nest in holes in trees; the woodpeckers, the starlings, nuthatch, redstart and even owls. Birds can't peck into the conifers – they are too sticky. On the other side, when the firs were planted and were still small, we had quite a lot of new birds we hadn't seen before. There were the tree-pipits, the reed-buntings, skylarks, nightjars, all of the birds who felt safer and snug in the thick low trees, where their enemies couldn't get at them. Another change soon after the felling of the big trees was the fields of foxgloves with which the whole place was carpeted. Then of course they disappeared again as the new trees are planted and grow. So do some of the birds. A lot of the tree pipits, which lay their eggs on the ground, have moved away again as the trees got thicker and higher.

"We'll take a walk around what they call Great Millhole. This side of the road, we'll be in the old woods, and you can enjoy the forest as it's been for hundreds of years. This here is probably part of the old track, where former Abergavennies would drive or ride from Eridge castle to Rotherfield church, the mother church for the whole district. They say that back in those days an Abergavenny could travel from Eridge to the coast without ever leaving his own property.

"You'll see a lot of the wood here has been coppiced. Do you know what I mean by that? Well, they do it with chestnut mostly, or perhaps hazel or ash. Every twelve or fourteen years you cut the wood right down practically to the ground. It's like all pruning. Then out of the roots it'll spread to four or five separate shoots. Then twelve or so years later you cut again, and more fresh shoots will sprout out at the bottom. So you get very thick growth you can use to make what we call spiles or poles, for fences and the like when you don't want big trees.

"Now let's take this other path. I want to show you something. Look at all those fungi. These big ones, the boletus, are edible. In fact a lot of the mushrooms you buy in tins at the grocers come from these. But there's another kind they call Devil's boletus, with a red stalk; that's poisonous. There must be hundreds of different kinds of toadstools in these woods alone. See this? It's the puffball. You've only just to touch it and it'll throw off its spores in a kind of dust cloud. Even a spatter of rain will set 'em going. Some of them can grow as big as a football. It's quite harmless, and they say you can eat it. Doesn't look very tempting.

"You'd better be on the safe side with fungi. There are one or two around here that are very poisonous, and for some there's no antidote. You get some beautiful fungi in groups and clusters. Look at those, just like a whole regiment of parachutes coming down together. That type only grow on dead beech wood, we call it the beech tuft. There's a pretty one, like a red icecream sundae, sprinkled with nuts. Don't touch it though. It could pretty near kill you, its the fly agaric.

"That fungus with the pretty flower-like shape and delicate apricot colour is called chanterelle. It smells of apricot too. It is quite safe to eat. So is the beefsteak fungus, growing on live or dead oak. If you cut them they bleed, and look for all the world like a fine piece of rare steak. I don't think much of the taste. The French like them and mess them up with a lot of garlic.

"But of course for me, the woods above all mean birds. One of the best experiences I ever had photographing birds in the old woods was when I spotted a kestrels' nest. Getting shots of the kestrel is quite a job. It was another of those ladder games. They like to nest high up, where they can scan the ground with those gimlet eyes of theirs and spot a mouse or even a beetle, and be down on it in a flash. Kestrels have been getting more common lately. One year I spotted a nest high up, and thought I'd try and get a series of shots as the eggs hatched and the young birds grew up. It meant carrying a long ladder nearly half a mile to the spot each time, and I'd go up the trees every three days or so.

"One day someone saw me setting off. 'Where are you going with that ladder?' 'Mushrooming' I said.

"Sometimes it was quite windy up that tree. In fact I had to tie two trees together to keep me and the camera steady. I was so near the birds that I had to grip with my knees and lean right back as far as I could, to get the birds in focus. I was only two or three feet away from them at times. The funny thing is they never took much notice of me. Kestrels can attack if they think you're interfering with their young. I wouldn't care for a kestrel coming at me like a jet plane. But they never did. They just got on with rearing a family and I got on with making them a photo album. So I got pictures of the babies from a week old, on through what I call the dirty stage, half feather and half fluff, until they were ready to fly. For some reason one of the young'uns stayed after the others had flown. We were staring right into one another's eyes at about two and a half feet, when I got my last picture. And what wonderful eyes!

"Over the road you get the newly planted part of the forest: spruce, fir and pine all in neat rows like soldiers on parade. They have made broad fire-breaks and trails where people can ride. There's plenty of heather and the bracken is growing fast. To start with they left some beeches, skyline beeches they called them, to improve the look of the place, but I notice they've cut most of them down now. They planted a nice lot of copper beech too. But while the trees were still young, some thief made away with the lot. You could still pull them out of the ground. I suppose they're making a nice hedge down someone's garden.

"Now they've stopped planting, and all the young firs and such have grown up pretty tall. There's views of Rotherfield Church we got when the trees were small, that no one will ever see again in our time. Several of the new birds that came when the firs were small have left us again. Now it's more pigeons and doves, and jays and bullfinches.

"Do you hear that noise? That's the greater spotted woodpecker tapping away. No, it's not building a nest. The nest's there already. That noise is more a warning signal. 'Keep out of my territory.' It uses that tapping other times for courting or it may be testing for a hollow sound. The young woodpeckers are so fierce and hungry, I've seen them push the parent bird right off the tree. The parent regurgitates to feed its young and it has to put its beak right down the littl'uns throat.

"The woodpeckers tap out a fresh nest every season. Other birds are not so particular. There was a starling for instance that took over a hole where I had photographed a green woodpecker the previous year. I think if you were to compare the pictures closely, you'd see it's first a woodpecker, and then a starling in the very same hole. A nuthatch will take over a ready-made hole in the same way, and then plaster it with mud to fit its size, and so keep a starling or some other intruder away.

"There's several different kinds of tits in the woods, the blue, great, willow tits and the rest. The willow tit is the only one that digs out its nest in rotten trees or stumps. The long-tailed tit is a wonderful builder. The nest is covered with lichens and cobwebs and lined with hundreds of feathers. It can lay up to a dozen eggs. I've seen a nest with a male and two females sharing it, and I don't know how many littl'uns. How they all get in at night is a mystery to me, with their long tails folded over one another. Talk about over-crowding. I saw one one evening and it was just solid black, not one speck of spare room. But they all seem to manage somehow. Another case of crowding is the wrens. They lay plenty of eggs and all crowd in together for protection in cold weather. The goldcrest is the smallest British bird, it doesn't weigh much more than an air letter. I got a picture of one with its little crest all puffed out. That's rare.

"There's an old woodman's hut down in the woods, where I found a beautiful wren's nest. It was built into a cart rope that had been nicely folded in a figure of eight. I took a photo of the nest and kept a lookout for the jenny wren to arrive. The cock wren builds the nest and he makes several of them and insists the female chooses which one she likes best. This cock had built several in the shed and when his mate came to inspect them the silly creature skipped the nice little nest in the rope, and chose a much rougher one attached to an old bit of hessian, such as they used to use in the hop gardens. It may have made more of a windbreak. It wasn't so good for the camera.

"You find the tree-creeper nesting in the crevices of trees. It's hard to spot because of camouflage, but it's for ever climbing up trees picking out insects with its long beak. It can climb up, but it can't climb down, so as soon as it finishes one course, it must fly down from the tree top, and begin another at the bottom of the next tree. The only bird of ours that regularly climbs down trees head-first is the nuthatch. That's a pretty bird, with colouring a bit like the kingfisher, only paler.

"You see the wood spurge growing along the side of the path. The flowers look like green leaves. You must know the lords and ladies,

parson in the pulpit is another name. He's dressed in a green and purple gown. A more correct name is cuckoo-pint. Later in the summer it comes out in red berries. Don't try and eat them, and don't let your children do it either. The saw-wort grows like a single thistle, but it doesn't have any prickles. The leaves are like the edge of a saw. It isn't so common, but you do find them around the woods and grasslands here. There's a very rare plant indeed grows just outside my patch. It's a simple green flower growing by the roadside, and it doesn't look much. But they protect it as best they can, and the Sussex Trust have put posts up to stop the hedge cutting machinery going over it. They are trying to get more to grow elsewhere. It's the spiked rampion. Of course what's common enough in one part of the country is unknown in another. I got a chance once to show some of my slides to members of the Quorn Hunt in Leicestershire. They were specially keen on my pictures of the common primrose. I was surprised to find that the primrose is pretty well unknown there."

So we went on exploring, but the shadows were lengthening now, and the sun was low shining through the branches, and the mist from the ground was making sunbeams. We turned for home.

The Walk Home

ON A walk Peter's usually too busy listening, looking, perhaps explaining to a friend what he hears and sees, to have time for much else. Besides he knows that if you are nature watching, it's often best to keep your mouth shut and let the wild life around you do the talking. But on the long walk home, as we both relax, enjoying slightly weary muscles, the leisurely pace, and the drawn-out summer daylight, Peter will sometimes unfold and share some of the thoughts and experiences of a true countryman.

"The thing about the country is that it's all there for you to find. Everything's free, if you know how to look. Why, in the town they are all in such a hurry they don't see anything. I don't think they'd be able to live if they didn't have a tin opener. I've had a good life. I don't crave anything. I like my work as a gardener. Mind you, in the old days, it wasn't always what it ought to have been. After my father died through an accident in the woods, I gave up the timber job and worked as garden boy in one of the big houses around here. 'Boy' they called it, though by that time I was a married man. I'd worked all week and then on Sunday morning we came in early and cleaned twenty or thirty pairs of shoes and boots, after the hunting and shooting the evening parties and the like. Then there'd be the fresh milk to fetch from the farm, the knives to clean maybe, and at the weekend you always had to polish and clean the marble statue of some family Baroness, or something. Afterwards the rest of the day was your own – that is till four o'clock when you went to fetch the cream and milk again for tea.

"There came a time when one of the gardeners left. Another fellow and I had been under him. We weren't earning much and, as our work grew, we thought we deserved a bit more, I being just married and all. So one Saturday morning we went to the master of the house and told him. He looked hard at us and then he said 'You're quite right. You do deserve more. Unfortunately I can't afford it. So I'll tell you what I'll do. I'll fire you both. Then you can go and find a better job.'

"That was the time I made up my mind I wasn't going to be tied to anyone for my living. I'd be my own boss. I'll do anything I can for someone who asks me to do it, but 'a Warnett can't be druv.' Same way, I don't want to drive anyone else. Two or three times during the war they wanted to give me a stripe, make me a corporal or something, but each time I got out of it. These men I was serving with were my friends. I just couldn't yell at them. That's why I became a jobbing gardener. It's one of the poorest paid jobs, but there are compensations. The old gentleman I worked for for three days a week for twenty-five years, he always said 'Grow enough for us, and then grow enough for you and your family as well.' So I had to try the first root of potatoes, didn't I? See if they were good all right. And the first picking of peas. There were apples pretty well all the year round, and bags of plums. We'd get strawberries to bottle. The wife always put one bottle of strawberries in syrup. That was for Christmas.

"The wife and I started out with nothing. I bicycled to my wedding. She and her sister came by bus. I took my bride home sitting on the handlebars of my bike.

"But after we were married we rented a cottage in Rotherfield, and there we stayed for forty years. I've managed to buy it now. We bought our furniture second-hand. Why, I've seen many a piece thrown out in the woods that was a sight better than we had. But one thing we could say, everything we owned was ours. We didn't have to go into debt, or beg for anything. My aim was to be just independent. There's an old Sussex saying 'You don't want to go hump-backed for your pension.' Stay upright, as long as you can. You don't need to be rich, but work hard and you can look the world in the face. Money doesn't bother me too much. Those that have too much seem to worry themselves sick in case they lose it.

"I don't worry about what I haven't got. I don't need one of those big cars that block the lanes. I've got my bike haven't I? Besides, feet are what you were born with. You may as well use them. You can dump your bike in the hedge, and walk in the woods. Beauty's there and it doesn't cost you a thing. Why in the town you even have to pay to park your car.

"Of course, these days my photography is expensive. But I don't smoke or drink, do I? As soon as I got to the legal age to smoke, I gave it up. It wasn't any fun any more. An awful lot of money goes up in smoke. I've got some lovely pictures to show for mine.

"And then you see, every year's different. I always carry a notebook and pencil with me when I go out, and jot down when I first see or hear a newcomer, or the return of an old one. Then I can compare this year with last. Why, only yesterday, walking with a friend in the woods, we saw something we'd never seen before, after all these years. They call it the lesser butterfly orchid. It's creamy white, and it was practically hidden underneath the bracken. Then on our special patch we saw three white admirals. They were settled on blackberry plants. That helps to camouflage their mottled white and brown.

"But the big thing this year so far has been the cuckoo. Cuckoos, like nightingales, have been very scarce lately. In fact I hadn't seen one for years. I had found a cuckoo's egg in a robin's nest, but the eggs got taken. Then there was one in a jenny wren's nest. That got taken by badgers. I saw one in a sparrow's nest. Two days later there was a big storm and the nest got washed away. Then this spring my nephew told me he'd heard a cuckoo singing regularly down in Holme Park woods. We went to look and I found a nest with one great beak in it. I think that will be the picture of the year for me.

"Since then we've put up hides at nests with cuckoos eggs. While we were there we heard a garden warbler and found that nest, and then we found the lesser whitethroat, so that brought us three birds.

"I suppose in the end it's a question of 'eyes and no eyes'. Or with me, to begin with it's more 'ears and no ears'. If you know how to listen you can place the sound and then you'll know where to look. Sitting quietly in one place may be better than walking about. And to go alone is better than going with a party, who may start chattering away. The wild life will hear you then long before you ever get to them. But you sit still maybe for twenty minutes or half an hour and you hear nothing, and then something happens. The other day I suddenly heard a couple of wrens giving sharp cries of alarm. I tracked them down to their nest in the heather. I looked inside. I'm glad I did rather than put a hand in, because there was an adder spread over it. It quickly made off, but there were three young ones dead. I felt underneath and there were two more alive, they managed to flutter away. The parents would go on feeding them and they probably recovered.

"I never get tired of the woods. I have a whole set of pictures of a single day from the first mist of dawn right through to the last glow of sunset. Then of course there are all the changes of season. Right now all that rich variety of different greens in spring has given way to summer when the green looks all much the same and the woods have lost their freshness. With autumn all the variety will come again, only this time it's the reds and browns and gold. Sometimes I think the frozen mist and hoarfrost of winter, picking out the bare branches, can be the most beautiful of all.

"Everything in nature is there and free, if you like to go out and look for it, and know how to behave yourself. We are apt to frown on town visitors who come down and leave gates open, spread litter, leave food about that may poison a bird or animal, throw cans and such into streams, pick rare plants, and take eggs from nests. When you come to think of it, a patch of woodland that seems so quiet and still, is the home of a huge population of living beings, that have been held in nature's balance for thousands of years. Interfere by introducing squirrels or minks, or by insecticide sprays or myxomatosis, and you may throw out that balance. Then you wonder why such and such a bird or butterfly has grown scarce, or whole species have disappeared. You may destroy the very thing you are trying to protect, by fencing it in. You may smother a delicate plant by allowing other things to grow that shouldn't be there.

"Our badgers aren't around just now. We have taken people to see them. Then some of those people think that they might go and look on their own. They are in too much of a hurry. They expect to get results in a couple of nights that have taken us several seasons to achieve, building up trust and getting ourselves accepted. Or on the other side you can make the badgers too friendly. I hear that now the badgers are following one fellow home and waiting at his door to be fed.

"Even your trained naturalist can get in the way. An old woodman down by the Hornshurst woods told me once he'd seen a strange bird so I went down and kept a look-out. First I heard the sound. *'Hoop, hoop, hoop.'* Then I saw the bird with its fan-shaped crest. It was a hoopoe. It comes originally from India and the middle-east, I'm told, though it sometimes passes through southern Britain on migration. Anyhow I reported it. Next thing I knew the big bird-watchers were all there in their cars, running around with their binoculars. Of course they drove it away. Nowadays I only report things after they're gone. You have to respect nature. Leave it alone as much as ever you can. It knows a lot of things better than what you do. After all with the flowers, the birds and the animals, it's their world as well as ours. Snatch nature for yourself and you'll lose it. Treat it right, and it will give you back a fortune."

Index

to colour photographs